WHERE THE JOBS ARE

Identification and Analysis of Local Employment Opportunities

William L. McKee
Richard C. Froeschle

1985

W. E. Upjohn Institute for Employment Research

Library of Congress Cataloging in Publication Data

McKee, William L.
  Where the jobs are.

  1. Job vacancies. 2. Job vacancies—Information
services. 3. Employment agencies. 4. Employment
forecasting. I. Froeschle, Richard C. II. Title.
HD5710.5.M38 1985   650.1'4   85-10570
ISBN 0-88099-028-7
ISBN 0-88099-029-5 (pbk.)

ROBERT MANNING
STROZIER LIBRARY

OCT 13 1986

Tallahassee, Florida

Soc
HD
5710.5
M38
1985

Copyright © 1985
by the
W. E. UPJOHN INSTITUTE
FOR EMPLOYMENT RESEARCH

300 South Westnedge Ave.
Kalamazoo, Michigan 49007

THE INSTITUTE, a nonprofit research organization, was established
on July 1, 1945. It is an activity of the W. E. Upjohn Unemployment
Trustee Corporation, which was formed in 1932 to administer a fund set
aside by the late Dr. W. E. Upjohn for the purpose of carrying on
"research into the causes and effects of unemployment and measures for
the alleviation of unemployment."

The Board of Trustees
of the
W. E. Upjohn
Unemployment Trustee Corporation

Preston S. Parish, Chairman
Charles C. Gibbons, Vice Chairman
James H. Duncan, Secretary-Treasurer
E. Gifford Upjohn, M.D.
Mrs. Genevieve U. Gilmore
John T. Bernhard
Paul H. Todd
David W. Breneman
Ray T. Parfet, Jr.

The Staff of the Institute

Robert G. Spiegelman, Director
Saul J. Blaustein
Judith K. Gentry
Phyllis R. Buskirk
H. Allan Hunt
Timothy L. Hunt
Robert A. Straits
Stephen A. Woodbury
Jack R. Woods

Authors

William McKee is director of the Institute of Applied Economics at North Texas State University. Dr. McKee received his Ph.D. in economics from the University of Missouri in 1975 and was a staff associate in employment policy at the Brookings Institution prior to his present position.

Richard Froeschle is currently a labor market information specialist for the Texas Department of Community Affairs. Among other responsibilities under the Job Training Partnership Act, Mr. Froeschle is responsible for planning and implementing a comprehensive local area LMI system in Texas. Upon completion of graduate work at North Texas State University, he joined the National Labor Market Information Training Institute where he served as in-service instructor and curriculum developer.

Foreword

An understanding of the structure and dynamics of the local labor market is a prime requisite for professionals involved in career counseling, curriculum development, policymaking and program planning at the local level. Such an understanding requires knowledge of the sources of labor market information and a practical method of data analysis.

There is a wealth of labor market information available to help the practitioner analyze local employment trends and projections and identify job opportunities that exist within local communities. The approach to applied labor market analysis presented in this monograph was designed for the nontechnical user of statistical data. It provides a detailed description of the sources of data and a step-by-step process for analysis and interpretation of data.

Facts and observations presented in this monograph are the sole responsibility of the authors. Their viewpoints do not necessarily represent positions of the W. E. Upjohn Institute for Employment Research.

Robert G. Spiegelman
Executive Director

Acknowledgments

We could not have undertaken this effort without the encouragement and assistance of the Employment Service research staff from state agencies across the country. These and other labor market information specialists have dedicated their careers to the provision of localized economic information.

Special thanks are due to Mark Hughes who stimulated the interest of both authors in the application of labor market information. William Luker enabled us to see the deeper relevance of intuitive analysis and also provided the framework for our presentation of the topic. Nancy Viens performed capably, as always, in typing endless drafts of the manuscript. All remaining errors are ours.

Preface

The purpose of this monograph is to provide the nontechnical user with an introduction to applied labor market analysis of local economic conditions. In particular, it presents a straightforward method for identifying and analyzing private sector job opportunities within a local community setting. The contents deal directly with the available sources of labor market information and provide the reader with a guide to accessing that data. To build understanding, the description of sources is undertaken within the context of an analytical framework useful in organizing and interpreting the variety of information items.

Labor market analysis, primarily because of its focus on economic data, is too often perceived as the exclusive domain of economists and statisticians. There is a need to make labor market information and analysis less complex. The intent here is to provide the layman with a guide for accessing the variety of available information and using the data in a meaningful way. It is hoped that, through this monograph, the less experienced data user can come to appreciate the wealth of information that can be used to identify the job opportunities that exist within local communities across the nation.

Unlike many handbooks dealing with occupational analysis or supply/demand information systems, this monograph presents an approach which enables the user to achieve an understanding of an integrated local labor market. This does not mean that the work is comprehensive in scope, particularly since several more quantitative techniques of regional economic analysis are not referenced. It is, however, organized in such a way that each subsection of the analysis fits into an examination of the labor market. The particular order of presentation is (1) conducive to understanding the structure of a local labor market and (2) realistic in terms of data readily available to the practitioner.

This treatment of labor market analysis follows an approach the authors have tested over several years. Despite its broad acceptance, other analysts recommend alternative starting points and methodological approaches to understanding the dynamics of the local labor market. It is not the intent of this discussion to discourage other analytical approaches. However, there are certain constraints in terms of data availability and timeliness, geographic considerations, and data classification issues which make the analytical structure followed here the most practical for most practitioners.

Because of shortcomings in the existing network of labor market information, no analysis of a local labor market can be totally accurate. Due to the absence of a unified theoretical framework for local labor market analysis, in conjunction with a fragmented data base, many observations must be generalized from prevailing economic and demographic trends and theories. Moreover, with imperfect measurement and sampling techniques and the time consuming nature of data collection, explanations of labor market phenomena are often based on hindsight, with some unavoidable imprecision.

It must be pointed out, however, that, although practitioners need to be aware of data limitations and theoretical imperfections in the methodology, analysts must do the best job with what is available. While acknowledging and dealing with inherent flaws in the information system, this monograph provides the practitioner with the background information and an analytical approach to understanding the dynamics of the local labor market and identifying existing job opportunities.

Despite recognized differences in data availability from state to state, there remains a core of information sources, both national and local, which can provide the basis for analysis. The data organization and analytical procedures presented here will aid the analyst in interpreting more expertly the available data and in achieving an understanding of the structure and dynamics of the local labor market.

This monograph is a thoroughly revised and expanded version of a less complete work, *Jobs in the Private Sector: Uses of Labor Market Information,* published by the U.S. Department of Labor in 1980. This earlier work was supported, in part, by grant funds provided by the Division of Labor Market Information, Employment and Training Administration, U.S. Department of Labor. As customary, but no less true in this case, responsibility for errors of commission or omission rests with the authors and certainly not the U.S. Department of Labor.

Executive Summary

The increasing complexities of modern business and government agency functions impose substantial requirements for detailed information on the operations of local labor markets. Legislation and court decisions, dealing with a multitude of objectives such as affirmative action and job creation strategies, have also heightened the demand for publicly available labor market information (LMI).

From the perspective taken here, LMI encompasses labor force information, occupational information, and information on where and how to find a job. Much has already been written about the computer or information "revolution" that is having dramatic impact on the society at large and the economy in particular. While recognizing these issues, this monograph does not provide a new information system for identifying and projecting where these changes are occurring now or will develop in the future. Rather, the authors encourage the optimal use of the *publicly available* information that, for the most part, is readily available for those who want to analyze a local labor market.

An indication of local jobs currently available and those that are expected to become open in the near future—including their wage rates and education, training, and experience requirements—is essential information that influences the decisions made daily by jobseekers, career and placement counselors, public and private policymakers, and others who are interested in improving the market system or their own current market status. This monograph provides a logical process for the use of labor market information in the following applications.

- *policy decisions* involving, for example, industrial development and strategies to assist the unemployed and economically disadvantaged;

- *planning* to identify current and future job needs that require specific education and training;

- *curriculum development* in public and proprietary schools, as well as in particular employment and training projects;

- *career counseling* for students making their initial education and career decisions in addition to those persons who voluntarily or by economic force are considering mid-career changes;

- *job development and placement* in specific occupations, industries, and firms;

- *job search* activities involving the identification of employers and industries where job openings of a specific skill category are expected to be available.

The monograph also addresses the inadequacies that abound in our current LMI system. Instead of expounding on the intellectual exercise of developing a comprehensive LMI system, however, the authors focus on making good use of that information that is available now and is expected to remain so in the future. An extensive table of sources of available LMI is presented in the appendix in order to facilitate their use by readers from diverse backgrounds and training.

In this form, the monograph serves as a reference manual for identifying where job opportunities in a local community are expected to arise. The process described here provides a means of answering several questions: What job opportunities are available locally? What occupations are needed? In what areas is there a high potential for job placement? What are the hiring requirements? The systematic analytical process for identifying job opportunities entails a careful study of local employment trends and projections—first at the industry level and then by occupation. The process focuses particular attention on those openings which are expected to occur through worker replacement needs, often overlooked by those who look toward "high growth" jobs.

Contents

Chapter 1
Introduction and Approach

Introduction

Information about job opportunities is essential in guiding the decisions of planners, educators, placement specialists, students, businessmen and women, job seekers, and others who contemplate becoming economically active in the marketplace. Understanding the specifics of employment and job openings in a community is an integral part of many local level decisions—for a student about to choose a college major or a local planning agency which has funding to establish a skill training program. To enhance such an understanding, this monograph provides a practical, step-by-step process for using *publicly available* information to analyze the local labor market. The process presented here may also be adjusted to serve very narrow needs, such as identifying local employers who hire workers in a particular occupational category.

For whatever purpose, to take full advantage of the available resources a user must have a grasp of the wide variety of data sources and the ways in which the data may be used to analyze labor market activity. The user should also understand the *labor market concepts* used in the analysis, including the various components of the labor force and the manner in which data are collected. (Appendix 1 provides definitions of the fundamental labor force concepts which the reader will encounter.)

1

Intuitive Analysis

The intuitive methodology described here actually evolves from a practical and applied approach to making the most complete use of available labor market data. The more pure econometric or mathematical statistics approach, alternatively, proceeds from exactly specified relationships such as independent random sampling, normality of distribution, and homogeneity of variance. From these and other abstractions and assumptions, the mathematical statistician constructs a formal model which hinges upon its own internal consistency.

Intuitive data analysis is more a framework within which information is "teased" from the available, imperfect data. While this approach utilizes and depends upon the findings of statistical theory, intuitive analysis also draws heavily on the researcher's past experiences with these and similar data, reasoned hunches, and (hopefully) good sense. Data analysis in this approach involves the search for indications rather than conclusions. To identify emerging job opportunities in the local area, the process may risk a greater possibility of error, but it capitalizes on its greater frequency of occasions where the right answer is suggested.

In some situations, particularly those involving economic estimates based on statistical surveys of smaller Metropolitan Statistical Areas (MSAs) and counties, the surveys' standard errors are so large relative to the groups' average that intuitive analysis permits a more reasonable estimate. In other words, while one advantage of random sample surveying is that the analyst can calculate the exact limits of the data (i.e., standard errors), these standard errors may be so large that a more intuitive analytical process holds at least as good or better prospect of reasonableness. Still, the integrity of intuitive analysis depends almost entirely upon the reasonableness with which it is deduced.

For other reasons, such as the negative correlation between survey sample size and the amount of nonrandom error, intuitive analysis also may be preferred to a purer statistical approach. In association, then, with the cost efficiencies of intuitive analysis, the less than statistically pure approach has advantages aside from the major reason that it is adopted for local labor market analysis—statistically precise data are not available, at least for the most part.

Background and Methods

An analysis of industrial employment can be undertaken with techniques ranging in complexity from intricate statistical models to simple descriptive examination. The available data, support resources, time constraints, and unique characteristics of the local labor market all play a part in determining the particular technique of analysis that is most appropriate in a given situation. In most cases, a methodical review of the available labor market information will point out specific industrial categories where employment activity and the possibility of job openings seem strongest. In some cases, however, a more rigorous analysis is necessary in order to understand the underlying causes of labor market activity.

Regardless of the mechanical complexity of the approach, the available techniques of analysis depend upon several indicators of job openings potential.

(1) When available, *new hire and worker accession rates* provide some of the best direct indicators of job openings activity and placement potential. Job openings can occur only through employment growth or vacancies created by labor turnover. Workers vacate jobs for many reasons, including quits, deaths, retirements, transfer or promotion. In most situations, the number of job openings

created by turnover exceeds those resulting from employment growth, and the rates at which these vacancies occur vary by industry and geographic area; thus, the new hire rate, representing accessions to job openings, is greater in some industries and labor markets than in others. By assembling data on the number of new hires and calculating new hire rates for separate industries, those that exhibit the greatest potential for job openings can be identified.

Information on new hires, the new hire rate and worker accessions are available in states participating in the Employment Service Potential (ESP) and the Employer Information Systems (EIS) projects. These projects utilize unemployment insurance records (filed with the employment service by all covered employers) to track individual employees by industry and employer. From these records, new hire data are available. Both the ESP and EIS programs are new, however, and data are generally available only for major U.S. industrial sectors and major industrial sectors within each state. Some pilot states have operational systems that provide detailed new hire rates for the state as well as substate areas. In most states, though, ESP and EIS information is limited, and the analyst must rely upon national rates as indicators of local industry new hires.

Data on new hires are important indicators of job openings potential, but, because current detailed data are unavailable for most states and local areas, other factors must be considered.

(2) *The employment level* within an industry is an important indicator of job openings activity. When actual counts of job vacancies and new hires are

unavailable, the level of employment (or size of an industry) can be used as an indicator of job openings activity. If worker separations can be assumed to be uniform across industries, the largest number of openings will occur within the industrial categories with the greatest employment. Because of the volume of employment in large industries, separations will create a larger number of openings. Stated simply, *most of the job openings due to turnover will occur in industries where most of the jobs are located.* Analysis based upon size alone, however, can be misleading, and employment levels as an indicator should be used in conjunction with other supporting information.

The *Standard Industrial Classification (SIC) Manual* provides a systematic code for collecting and tabulating data by industry. This system promotes the uniformity and comparability of data collected by various governmental agencies and private organizations. Industries are classified by the type of activity in which they are engaged; thus, the classification system attempts to cover the entire field of national and local economic activities.

For the classification, an establishment is an economic unit, generally at a single physical location, where services or production are performed. The structure of the classification makes it possible to tabulate, analyze, and publish establishment data on a major division or on a two-digit, three-digit, or four-digit industry code basis according to the level of industrial detail considered most appropriate. Each establishment is assigned an industry code on the basis of its primary activity which is determined by its principal product or service rendered.

The major divisions are as follows:

- Agriculture, Forestry and Fishing
- Mining
- Construction
- Manufacturing
- Transportation and Public Utilities
- Wholesale Trade
- Retail Trade
- Finance, Insurance and Real Estate
- Services
- Public Administration
- Nonclassifiable establishments

Within each division, industrial detail is further disaggregated, thereby increasing the specificity of coverage within the industry. For example, Electrical and Electronic Equipment is classified as major group 36 within the major division of Manufacturing. Within SIC 36 there exist listings of industries at a more specified level of detail. SIC 363, for example, is the industry group Household Appliances. Within SIC 363 are still more detailed industries; SIC 3634 is Electrical Housewares and Fans. The hierarchy begins at the major division level and proceeds to two-, three-, and four-digit categories based on increasing specificity.

Data on employment by industry are readily available for most local areas. Within the public employment service (ES), the ES-202 record of employees covered by unemployment insurance provides a timely count of payroll employment by detailed industrial category within each state and county. In addition, the Current Employment Statistics survey (or 790 Program) operated by the ES estimates the number of employees on nonagricultural payrolls each month in each metropolitan area. Local industrial employment is recorded and published by several other resource agencies, including the U.S. Bureau of the Census and the Bureau of Economic Analysis, as well as many others.

(3) *Changes in employment* among different industries can provide a valuable indication of job openings activity in two ways. Obviously, net additions to employment evidence job openings within the industry. By monitoring employment changes, it is possible to identify industries in which new jobs are being added to the employment pool.

A second way in which this information is a useful indicator is that it contributes to identification of the direction of change of an industry's employment level and new hire rate. The employment level and new hire data are indicators of job openings activity, but they are measured for static moments in time. Data collection and dissemination take time. It may be feared that, by the time the data are actually in-hand, they may have become out-of-date and no longer represent an industry's current activity. Still, since up-to-the-minute data are unavailable, past and projected employment trends provide an understanding of whether an industry is generally advancing or declining. Recognizing the direction of change helps anticipate whether the number of job openings is expanding or contracting within an industry. In addition to historical time series, projections of future employment by industry are regularly produced by the ES for each state and major area.

(4) *The number of local establishments* (firms) in different industrial categories can be a useful indicator supplementing other information on job

openings activity. New hires and employment levels provide measures of the volume of job openings but do not lend insight into the nature of their hiring activities. Examining the number of establishments along with their levels of employment can pinpoint the industrial identification and concentration of large and small employers. This distinction is critical, since larger employers may have different hiring patterns and employment needs than smaller employers.

Data on the number of employing establishments, like employment data, are available from the ES as well as from other government agency sources. The ES-202 record provides a count of establishments reporting employment covered by unemployment insurance and can provide the number of establishments by size of employment. In addition, several sources available from the U.S. Bureau of the Census provide information on the number and size of employers in separate industry categories.

Analytical Process

The following analytical constructs provide (1) a sequential organization and (2) an analytical framework for using available labor market information (LMI) to identify potential job openings. Basically, the analysis of job opportunities proceeds from industries to occupations, using growth and replacement needs as signals indicating where openings can be expected. Since jobs originate from economic activity, the job search process begins by isolating the key industries in which, based on the analysis of available LMI, possibilities of job openings seem most likely. The key industries are those industries with the larger growth and replacement needs. Then, with specific key industries in mind, LMI can be used to search for jobs among the occupations associated with employment in those industries. Again, growth and replacement needs are indicators for analyzing occupations and identifying areas where job openings seem likely. As with industries, the prospects for openings in some occupations will be greater than in others.

Having identified industries and related occupations where job openings seem most likely, the background is established for measuring job quality and placement potential and for contacting related employers. Measuring job quality and placement potential involves collecting available LMI on training and education requirements, expected wage rates, and the potential supply of workers available to compete for those openings. With this more comprehensive view of potential job openings, employers may then be contacted in order to verify the anticipated opportunities in each occupational area. The industrial identification of key leading industries serves as a guide to those employers in which openings are expected to exist.

A more detailed examination of the use of available LMI to identify job openings is covered in the following chapters, but figure 1-1, "Labor Market Analytical Process," and the accompanying narrative outline the suggested procedure for identifying local job opportunities.

Step 1. Identify the geographic labor market

The initial step in the job identification process involves identifying the geographic jurisdiction of the local labor market. While the area of immediate interest may be a central city or county, identifying and understanding job opportunities can only be undertaken within the larger context of the geography of economic activity that generates employment. With few exceptions, that economic activity is contained in a geographic area somewhat larger than the city or

Figure 1-1
Labor Market Analytical Process

	Activity	Key Elements of Activity
Step 1	identify geographic labor market	• determine the political or economic jurisdiction • consider all significant pockets of job opportunity
Step 2	identify industrial structure of employment	• identify industrial composition • identify employment levels of industries • identify firms, employment class size
Step 3	analyze historical employment trends	• identify past patterns of growth (long term) • identify recent historical trends in employment
Step 4	interpret current economic conditions	• examine current industrial indicators of performance • compare employment levels with labor force participation
Step 5	inspect other current labor market indicators	• examine local job openings data • examine other local wage and hiring information
Step 6	incorporate employment projections	• examine absolute growth and decline projections • examine percent changes in projected employment
Step 7	rank local industries based on employment potential	• use the industrial evaluation model • identify specific two- and three-digit growth industries
Step 8	identify local employers	• identify local employer names by SIC industry category
Step 9	analyze the occupational composition of selected industries	• identify occupational staffing pattern of key selected industries examine employment distribution among occupations
Step 10	analyze occupational projections	• examine absolute projected employment increases • examine percent increases in projected employment
Step 11	consider job quality	• identify qualitative aspects of an occupation • consider skill transferability, job duties, wages and hours, working conditions, hiring requirements

county. It is important not to stratify the geographic area too narrowly, since it is possible to exclude important components contributing to employment and providing job opportunities.

The labor market area (LMA) and the metropolitan statistical area (MSA) are premised on concepts of economic activity and are logical geographic building blocks for labor market analysis. Both the LMA and MSA are defined by the relationship between place of residence and place of work of the labor force. The primary consideration involves the ability of workers to accept new jobs without the necessity of changing residences or incurring unreasonable commuting distances. To avoid fragmented, incomplete interpretations of job activity, analysis should, as a rule, first be conducted at the LMA or MSA geographic level. Then, analysis for smaller jurisdictions can be performed within that context.

Step 2. Identify the industrial structure of employment

Having identified the geographic area for analysis, the job identification process turns to gaining familiarity with (1) the industrial composition of the area, (2) employment levels among industries, and (3) employers among industries. The size of an industry and the number of employers within an industry can serve as an initial guide to key industries, since openings created by labor turnover and worker separations will occur within all industries. If separation rates are uniform across industry classifications, the largest number of openings should occur within the largest industrial categories (those with the highest employment levels). Because of the volume of employment in large industries, separations will create a large number of openings. From that view, large industries, or industries with large establishments, can be considered key leading industries.

Step 3. Analyze historical employment trends

After the user becomes familiar with the current structure of local industrial employment, the next step in the search for employment potential focuses on growth and growth trends. Specifically, it is important to know where growth has occurred in the past for purposes of understanding or projecting continued growth trends. Base and target years selected for this analysis are those that seem to best fit the trend of total industrial employment over the past five or so years. Then, simple calculations identify the absolute and percentage change in employment by industry. By examining the historical trends of each industry's employment, it is possible to identify industries that have experienced the greatest absolute growth or the fastest rise (percentage increase) in employment. Similarly, industries are identified which have large numbers of employees, yet are actually declining.

Step 4. Interpret current economic conditions of area industries

Although it is necessary to identify industries that have grown in the past, it is equally important to determine how those industries are functioning in the more recent time period. A good place to begin is with the state or local *Labor Market Information Newsletter* published by the local ES. The newsletter provides a narrative analysis of Current Employment Statistics (CES) data on employment trends and the number of nonagricultural wage and salary jobs by major two-digit (SIC) industry. Through a comparison of the figures for the recent month and for the same month in the previous year, it provides insight into how industry employment has expanded or contracted over the past year. Also included in the newsletter are CES data on average earnings and average hours worked, which, when tracked over several months, can be good leading indicators of the growth or decline of an industry.

Step 5. Inspect other current labor market indicators

There are other valuable data items, such as employment service job openings, for examining recent industrial trends. It is valuable to examine the ESARS (Employment Security Automated Reporting System) tables to identify current openings registered by industry to determine if there is an expressed demand for workers in those industries.

Step 6. Incorporate employment projections in the analysis

After examining the current industrial structure and recent and historical trends by industry, inspecting industry employment projections provides a future perspective of the industrial structure. Employment projections show employment data by industry for a base year, a current estimated year, and a target year so that it is possible to calculate absolute and percentage change, and, thereby, identify where the greatest amount of industrial growth is expected to occur. Another valuable source for understanding industrial projections is the *Industrial Outlook Handbook,* which provides a compact survey of U.S. industries and an overview of domestic and international developments which will influence their growth potential.

Step 7. Rank local industries according to their employment potential

The process in steps 1 through 6 above leads to the narrowing of an expansive local industrial structure to a few key industries which are more easily analyzed. This narrowing process continues to a finer level of industrial detail so that the final result is the identification of specific three- or four-digit SIC code industries which have exhibited past growth and are projected to continue growing.

In an analysis of the available local LMI, there normally will be a limited number of industries that consistently stand

out as healthy with good employment growth potential.
Replacement needs must also be considered, but data on
localized replacement needs are not generally available (except for special studies). For this reason, the discussion here
is premised on the assumption that replacement needs occur
uniformly across industries; thus, industry size can be used
as a measure of replacement need, and large industries can
be expected to experience a larger absolute volume of
replacement need. Combining replacement information with
growth data will highlight several key leading industries
which exhibit the greatest potential for employment.

Step 8. Identify local employers

After identifying specific four-digit industries with good
growth potential, it is a simple task to refer to a local Directory of Manufacturers, Dun and Bradstreet listing of million
dollar or middle-level firms, or a Chamber of Commerce
listing of local manufacturers, to get names, addresses, and
marketing scopes of individual firms within those industries.
Integrating this statistical overview of the sources of industrial employment with a general understanding of the
local employment structure, it is often more effective to contact those firms first before expanding the analysis.
Employer contact is essential because secondary data
systems universally are restricted in the nature and degree of
intensive, current information that can be collected through
either a survey or administrative reporting process.

Step 9. Analyze the occupational composition of selected industries

The next logical step, then, is to identify the occupations
(in relative terms) that comprise the workforce of each
selected industry. Again, the process of examining all the individual occupations within an industry will be aided by
reviewing the available LMI and identifying those occupations that represent the greatest reasonable expectation for

employment. When performing a local area economic analysis, disproportionately greater attention must be paid to expanding occupations within expanding industries (all other factors considered equal). If industries within the local area are not expanding, then job stability becomes the primary criterion.

The questions that need to be answered concerning occupations are: (1) How many jobs are there in each occupation within the key industries? (2) What occupations have the largest number of jobs in those industries? and (3) In which occupations are future job opportunities most likely to occur? The occupational composition of employment within industries, taken from the Occupational Employment Statistics (OES) program, will help determine the occupations making up employment within a particular industry and their percentage distributions. Although data on industry staffing patterns are usually available at the state level only, it is feasible to apply those same staffing patterns to the local area. Staffing patterns provide percentage distributions of major occupational groups; thus, it is possible to identify the most commonly reported occupations within the industry. In other words, some percentage of all the local firms within an industry will report jobs in similar occupational categories. This information, coupled with staffing pattern data, provides insight into the number of jobs within a given occupation in a given industry.

Step 10. Analyze occupational projections

Occupational projections are invaluable in identifying growth occupations by industry. Although some states are still using census-based projections, many states now have projections available from the Occupational Employment Statistics (OES) survey program. These projections result from multiplying total employment projections (for an industry in a target year) by industrial staffing ratios. By using the Industry/Occupation (I-O) matrix to cross-tabulate industrial employment estimates with occupational staffing patterns, it is possible to calculate the additional employment that will be necessary to satisfy occupational growth and replacement requirements.

Step 11. Consider job quality

It is not sufficient, though, to restrict analysis to only the number of jobs within an occupation. Rather, to facilitate the best match between workers and jobs, it is necessary to assess the quality of available jobs. In training or counseling individuals for specific occupations, it is important to analyze the nature of a given job according to: (1) transferability of skills within an occupation; (2) job duties and functions; (3) basic hiring requirement (including ports of entry); (4) pay range or average wage rates; and (5) firm-specific training requirements of potential employees. The task of assessing the quality of occupations becomes a two-fold process of reviewing and analyzing available LMI and gathering qualitative information through contacts with local employers.

The goal of identifying stable or expanding industries should always be kept in mind. Changes in economic trends or industrial structure, however, may require workers to transfer from one industry to another. By providing individuals with skills that are transferable among industries, there is greater probability that these workers will be able to achieve continuous employment.

The basic duties and functions associated with occupational categories can be obtained from any of the occupational classification manuals. The most detailed system is the *Dictionary of Occupational Titles (DOT)*. The *DOT* describes general tasks involved in the occupation, fields of specialization within an occupation, and identification of duties required of workers in this occupation. Another system is the *Standard Occupational Classification System (SOC)*.

There is no substitute for direct employer contact in gathering information on the last category—the firm's specific training requirements. While the majority of actual training takes place on the job, by contacting the individual employer one can learn what types of training are required for workers in that firm's entry level positions.

To achieve the greatest return on counseling, job search or training investments, it is important to identify not only the capabilities and needs of the individual, but also the quality, potential, and limitations of the occupation. If the best match between the individual and available jobs is facilitated, the resulting placement will be suited to the worker's needs, length of tenure on the job will increase, and further benefits will accrue to society. Ideally, identifying those occupations with the greatest employment potential and combining that knowledge with an understanding of job quality within occupations provides the counseling, training, and placement processes with better probabilities of success.

Chapter 2
Geography of Labor Markets
A Spatial Element

Introduction

Before performing local area economic analysis, several decisions must be made to establish the parameters of the study. Pertinent issues to be addressed in this beginning stage include: (1) the time frame under consideration, (2) the data sources to be employed, (3) the methodologies to be applied, and (4) the geographic area to be analyzed. Because a local labor market can be defined according to occupational, industrial or geographic considerations, the objectives of the study must be firmly in mind before analysis is begun.

Whereas the study of occupations and industries generally involves discussions of mobility or transferability across geographic regions, the study of the geography of a particular labor market is concerned with the spatial element of all economic activity within a certain locale. Specifically, geographic consideration of a labor market introduces the physical or spatial realities in regard to where people live and work. The geography of a labor market includes such elements as natural boundaries or configurations which direct or constrain economic or population expansion, the historical development patterns of the urban area, residential or industrial zoning decisions, and the extent and nature of the transportation network. These and other considerations

19

help to explain the location phenomena of where people live and work and the spatial barriers they confront.

The designation of an appropriate geographic area is an important decision. All too often in the study of economic activity, the spatial realities of a geographic area are overlooked. Because the economic interrelationships between geographical and political areas are complex, it is essential to understand these economic ties in order to appreciate fully how and why the local labor market functions as it does. If a labor market area is too narrowly defined, the analyst may get only a fragmented area that is not truly reflective of the employment, commuting, and income-generating patterns of the local area. Conversely, if the labor market area is too broadly defined, analysis may reveal socioeconomic or political forces that are at work in the larger area but which have minimal impact on the local area. In identifying and understanding the economic interrelationships which have shaped the local labor market, the possibility for anticipating change is increased.

Concentrations of industrial activity arise for a variety of reasons, not the least of which is the physical environment which constrains the human population to form a network of residential and industrial locations. Such factors as commuting times and distances and the availability and ease of mass transportation affect the development of a local labor market.

Labor Markets

The notion of a market, in economic terms, refers to the "place" where goods and services are exchanged (the product market) or where the factors of production, including labor, are acquired in exchange for money income (factor market). Although the *market,* in an economic sense, is an abstract term, a *labor market,* in reality, is generally a geographic area in which individuals sell their labor in return for money. The distance which an individual is willing to commute physically in order to sell his labor becomes the boundary of his labor market. When the travel to work decisions of a large group of individuals are combined, the physical boundaries of the collective labor market area can be delineated.

In defining a labor market area, the Department of Labor employs commuting time and distance factors in combination with certain density criteria. A labor market area is thus defined as that geographic area in which a concentration of workers can live, work, and change jobs without changing residences. Commuting patterns are the products of population flows into and out of local communities along major transportation routes. The type of transportation system (i.e., private automobile, bus, ferry, etc.) and the degree to which it is used (amount of congestion) affect the time of commuting and, therefore, the boundaries of any given labor market area.

To understand fully the relationship between where people live and work, it is important to comprehend the spatial elements of the geographic market place. Origin and destination studies conducted by federal or state transportation offices provide data on traffic flows between residential and commercial areas. In this way, the required time to travel to work can be calculated for large concentrations of individuals, and the labor market area can be specified.

Political Versus Economic Definitions of a Geographic Area

Geographic areas can be broadly grouped into two types: (1) those jurisdictions established for political and legislative needs, and (2) those divisions based on economic, social, physiographic, or cultural criteria. These general categories cover most geographic area definitions.

Since the boundaries of a political division may cut across or overlap the boundaries of several geographic areas defined according to some economic or social criteria, many academic and business disciplines have created their own geographic typologies. Most often, such classification systems are according to definitions which correspond closely to criteria unique to the particular discipline. Two good examples are (1) the field of transportation planning, which divides the country into daily urban systems (DUS) based on commuting patterns, and (2) the U.S. Postal System, which separates the nation by zone improvement plan (ZIP) codes based on mail volume.

Data systems based on political designations are created because of legal mandates which require data to be collected for the purposes of apportionment in legislative bodies, federal and state revenue sharing programs, and other administrative purposes. Data for state and substate areas are also necessary for governments to study the internal distribution of the population and labor force in relation to economic and social facilities and to identify changing patterns in migration. These data are, in turn, useful in policy decisions regarding planning for the location of economic development projects, as well as for a vast number of other social and economic concerns. The Bureau of the Census is responsible for collecting data for the federal government and, in that capacity, has created a geographic hierarchy by which it enumerates the U.S. population. State, county, and municipal governments similarly have been required to acquire data on the population and local economies within their prescribed geographic boundaries. As a consequence, there is a considerable amount of data collected for a myriad of legislative or political projects covering a large array of geographic areas. To illustrate this diversity, the "New York Region" once covered 42 cities, 22 county governments, 117 towns, 81 townships, 148 boroughs, 151 villages, and numerous authorities and interstate commissions.

For the purpose of studying geographic labor markets, the number of political/geographic areas can be narrowed to a few key jurisdictions. Beginning with the greatest degree of aggregation, a study may be done at the *national* level using data collected for the United States as a whole. Although the Census Bureau also has divided the country into four regions and nine divisions, the next largest geographic area for which significant amounts of data are available is the *state.* At the substate level, there are several political jurisdictions for which data are collected. Each state is divided into *counties* which represent the smallest geographic areas for which a large and diverse amount of data is collected. Most of the major data programs recognize the county as a significant geographic building block for which to provide data. For areas smaller than the county, the amount of available data, aside from the decennial census and local administrative records, falls off considerably. Below the county level are *cities* and *townships,* which are further subdivided into *census tracts* and *blocks.* Data which cover geographic areas of this size tend to be expensive to collect and are most often subject to large degrees of sampling error. The decennial census collects selected data for these areas, but little else is regularly available at this level.

Economic Areas

For many purposes, data are needed for areas other than those recognized as political jurisdictions. Nonpolitical areas in common use for statistical data gathering may be combinations or subdivisions of specified political areas. The major objective in defining an area based on some specific, nonpolitical criterion is to identify and isolate the relative economic homogeneity within the area. For the purpose of analyzing a labor market, several geographic jurisdictions are defined which reflect both the economic interdependence of industries within a given area and the relationship between the residence of the area's labor force and places of employment.

There are only two designations of labor market areas currently in use: (1) small LMAs and (2) major LMAs. Small labor market areas are defined as having a central community and surrounding territory which do not meet the standards for size or metropolitan character specified for major LMAs. They must include a town or city which acts as the "employment nucleus" of the area, but are not required to include whole counties which may or may not overlap into major labor market areas.

Major labor market areas are those which have a central city (or adjoining cities) with a population or 50,000 or more as designated by the U.S. Bureau of the Census. With few exceptions, major LMAs correspond with Metropolitan Statistical Areas (MSAs) as specified by the Office of Federal Statistical Policy and Standards. Also with few exceptions (New England is defined by towns), MSAs are comprised of counties as thier major building blocks. Although an MSA may cross state boundaries, it must include or exclude whole counties rather than only portions of a county, so the political integrity of the county unit is maintained.

A number of considerations were involved in the original establishment of the metropolitan statistical areas. Most important was the need for having local economic and social statistical data collected by government and private agencies presented on a common geographic basis to facilitate comparative analyses and other uses of the data. The areas were designed to serve a variety of statistical purposes, including local labor market analysis.

For each decennial census period the definitions and criteria for MSAs are reevaluated and revised. The 1980 Census was no exception, and several changes have been introduced into the concepts and definitions of an MSA.

Urban Development and Land Use Patterns

In addition to its physical boundaries and transportation network, the historical growth patterns of an area affect the relationship of where people currently live and work within the labor market area. Three concepts commonly are used to explain the spatial design and development of an urban area: (1) the concentric zone concept, (2) the sector concept, and (3) the multiple-nuclei concept (figure 2-1). Each of these concepts reflects the actual historical development of a particular urban area; however, the theories behind each concept serve more for description of urban land use patterns than as classifications of urban development. Most cities generally conform to some extent to one of these land use patterns.

The concentric zone concept first identifies a *central core* or downtown business district surrounded concentrically by rings of land, each representing a distinct zone within the city. Moving outward from the core, the first ring is the *zone of transition* which is characterized by its diversity of functions but is usually an older and often decaying residential area. The second ring is a continuation of the downtown residential district and is referred to as the *zone of working men's homes*. (This area often is ringed by a thin band of retail shopping areas and industrial parks referred to as the *ancilliary business district*.) These decentralized commercial areas are surrounded by the final two zones, both suburban: the *zone of better residences* and the *commuter's zone*. Residential neighborhoods are likely to spring up in these suburban rings along major freeways and mass transit routes which provide access to downtown business areas.

In contrast to the simplified concentric zone concept, the sector concept describes a pattern of development in which wedge-shaped sectors of peripheral residential areas surround the central business district and move outward. The

Figure 2-1

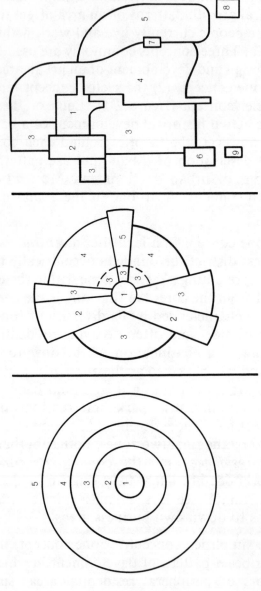

CONCENTRIC CONCEPT
1. Central business district
2. Zone of transition
3. Zone of workingmen's homes
4. Zone of better residences
5. Commuter's zone

SECTOR CONCEPT
1. Central business district
2. Wholesale and light manufacturing
3. Low-class residential
4. Middle-class residential
5. High-class residential

MULTIPLE-NUCLEI CONCEPT
1-5. Same as sector concept
6. Heavy manufacturing
7. Outlying business district
8. Residential suburb
9. Industrial suburb

SOURCE: Chauncy Harris and Edward Ullman, "The Nature of Cities." *Annals of the American Academy of Political and Social Science* 242: 6 (1945).

wedge-shaped zones represent sectors of different income classes which tend to emanate outward from the center to the periphery along major transportation routes. In other words, lower-priced residential areas occupy entire sectors of the city, from the center to the suburbs. Similarly, higher-priced areas tend to be not only in suburban areas but begin in luxury high rises downtown and move outward to affluent urban and suburban neighborhoods.

The third theory, known as the multiple-nuclei concept, appears more in line with the realities of contemporary metropolitan land use patterns. Instead of focusing on one downtown central business district, this theory contends that suburban decentralization and the rise of shopping malls and industrial parks create several new growth centers around which residential and retail building grow. Such growth is based on the interdependence of several key industries which become mutually self-supporting and engender additional residential growth. The rise of additional commercial cores causes the surrounding territory to be filled, depending on the tradeoffs between the cost and availability of both land and transportation.

Selected Chapter Bibliography

Berry, Brian, editor. *City Classification Handbook: Methods and Applications.* New York: John Wiley and Sons, 1972.

Chapin, F. Stuart. *Urban Land Use Planning.* Chicago: University of Illinois Press, 1979.

Johnson, James J. *Urban Geography: An Introductory Analysis.* London: Pergamon Press, 1967.

Johnston, R.J. *The American Urban System: A Geographical Perspective.* New York: St. Martin's Press, 1982.

Lansing, John B. and Eva Mueller. *The Geographic Mobility of Labor.* Ann Arbor: Institute for Social Research, 1973.

Palm, Risa. *The Geography of American Cities.* New York: Oxford University Press, 1981.

Perloff, Harvey. *How a Region Grows: Area Development in the U.S. Economy.* New York: Committee for Economic Development, 1963.

Schreiber, Arthur, Paul Gatons and Richard Clemmer. *Economy of Urban Problems: An Introduction.* Boston: Houghton Mifflin, 1976.

Smith, David. *Industrial Location: An Economic Geographical Analysis.* New York: John Wiley and Sons, 1971.

Smith, Wallace F. *Urban Development: The Process and the Problems.* Berkeley: University of California Press, 1975.

Sternlieb, George and James Hughes, editors. *Post-Industrial America: Metropolitan Decline and Inter-Regional Job Shifts.* New Brunswick: Center for Urban Policy Research, 1975.

U.S. Department of Labor, Employment and Training Administration. *Why Families Move.* Washington: Government Printing Office, 1977.

U.S. Department of Labor, Employment and Training Administration. *Directory of Labor Market Areas.* Washington: Government Printing Office, 1980.

Weinstein, Bernard and Robert Firestone. *Regional Growth and Decline in the United States.* New York: Praeger Publishers, 1978.

Chapter 3
Local Area
Industrial Analysis

Introduction

The process of identifying key leading industries in a local economy is fundamentally intuitive research, based on a combination of quantitative analyses with applications of qualitative factors. Although the ultimate selection of those industries with the greatest potential for job openings must be tempered by the analyst's local experience and best judgment, basic industrial analysis is dependent on the interpretation and synthesis of various economic indicators and appropriate statistical data.

The process of prioritizing the industrial sectors of the local economy according to job opening potential hinges on relative decisions. To select one industry over another does not mean that there is not job opening potential in the other industry; rather, the selected industry has a relatively greater potential for job openings or potential for a greater number of job openings of a particular type. The final step in the analysis is to develop a summary table which allows the analyst to identify, on a relative basis, those industries with the greatest promise for future job openings. A ranking of these industries will result in a priority listing of industrial sectors expected to provide the greatest job opening poten-

29

tial, thus increasing the effectiveness of placement counseling, employer contact, and job development activities.

This direct approach to identifying key leading industries makes full use of available data. The time required to collect and interpret the requisite data is minimized, and most of the quantitative methods employed are no more complex than simple percentage changes and basic algebraic manipulations. By using such a process, randomness is reduced in planning and job counseling activities. For job development purposes, increased effectiveness results from concentrating valuable time on employers in key leading industries rather than on those in declining industrial sectors. Still, it should be noted that this approach may need to be modified to meet the specific needs of individual users, and that alternative approaches are available for adoption.

Industry analysis can be used for a variety of purposes not limited to identifying growth industries in a regional development or planning context. It provides valuable information for economic development efforts to diversify an area's economic base or to encourage expansion of those key industries which attract exogenous income and stimulate employment. It may also form the initial step in human resource planning, whereby the ultimate design is to identify occupations with skill shortages and provide job or career training programs to meet both individual and societal needs. Whatever the objective, this approach to developing an understanding of local labor market conditions is a building block for initiating employer contact, manpower planning, job development, and other labor market projects.

Analytical Process

The approach presented here focuses on the organization and interpretation of labor market information and is consistent with theoretical concepts of how job openings occur.

This sequential process consists of (1) an analysis of the current industrial structure of the local area to identify the industries (by their relative sizes) which comprise the local economy; (2) an assessment of the change in industry employment over a recent historical period; (3) an examination of projected trends in industry employment; (4) an analysis of current employment trends, including an examination of recent layoffs and plant closings, average hours worked, weekly earnings, and job openings by industrial category; (5) a synthesis of data from the various steps, resulting in the development of a priority listing of key leading industries, and (6) a listing of employers (by size class) which make up those industries identified in step 5. The approach presented in this chapter demonstrates an effective method to collect, review and analyze industry data in a systematic fashion. (This process has also been programmed for personal computers. A detailed discussion of the *Industrial Evaluation Model* is presented in appendix 3.)

To clarify the process, the following sections present an analysis of a sample study area—Travis County, Texas. Study of the local industrial base will use data collected and classified under the Standard Industrial Classification (SIC) coding system (see chapter 1). For pedagogical purposes, the concentration of this analysis will be at the major division SIC level of detail, with two-digit detail for manufacturing industries. This is done strictly for purposes of illustration. For most applied uses, a complete analysis should include detailed data for all industry sectors, particularly when larger, more diversified economic areas are under study.

Step 1
Current Industrial Structure

As specified in the description of the analytical process, an industrial analysis begins with an overview of the area's current economic structure. Before identifying where current and expected job opportunities may occur, it is important to understand the size, diversification, and nature of the existing local economy. This preliminary step is very important to the analytical process because, as in any regional analysis, the trends and dynamics of the local economy are much more apparent if the researcher has a firm understanding of the existing local economy. The activities at this stage involve assessing:

- current levels of employment among industry categories;
- the number of establishments within those industries; and
- the concentration and relative size of industries in the local economy.

Issues

Some questions posed at this juncture might include:

(1) How many total employees are there in the local area?
(2) What industries (by SIC code) comprise the local economy?
(3) How many workers does each industry employ?
(4) Which industries are the largest in terms of employment, of value added, and of sales volume?
(5) How many establishments (firms) are in each industry?
(6) Which industries have the largest number of establishments?
(7) Which industries have the greatest concentration of larger firms (20 or more employees)?
(8) Which industries have the largest coefficients of specialization?
(9) Which are the base industries in the local economy (i.e., coefficients of specialization greater than one)?
(10) Does the local area have a diversified economic base or is it dependent on only one or two industries?

The answers to these questions provide the analyst with a basic understanding of the structure of the local economy. Additional perceptions that the analyst develops while working through the data tables will serve to augment the analysis. Similarly, the analyst's experience and intuitive knowledge of local area conditions should be incorporated into the analysis.

Data Sources

There are several data sources which can be used to assess the current industrial structure of a local area. Each data source has both benefits and drawbacks. The Employment Security Agency (ES) in each state has an economic research and statistics (analysis) division which administers the *Current Employment Statistics* (CES) Program. (It is also referred to as BLS-790 data by many users.) This is a monthly survey sample of employers within the state and provides statewide and metropolitan area data on the level of employment and average hours and earnings by SIC industry category. Although it is the most current employment data, with a lag time of roughly one month, it does not provide sufficient industrial detail for many projects nor is it available at the substate level, other than for major metropolitan areas.

The ES-202 program, commonly referred to as Covered Wages and Employment, is the most comprehensive source of industry employment data available at the substate level. These data are taken from quarterly unemployment insurance (UI) records and provide detailed employment by industry, number of reporting units, and total wages data. Despite the strictly enforced federal laws prohibiting disclosure of data which could possibly identify any single employer, most ES-202 data can be made available by the ES on a county basis at the three-digit SIC level of detail. The ES-202 data tend to become available with lag of six to nine months.

A third source of industry employment data comes from the Department of Commerce publication, *County Business Patterns*. This publication provides nonagricultural industry employment, number of business establishments by employer size class, and industry payroll data for each county in the U.S. (with a separate publication for each state). These data are published at the four-digit SIC level. However, due to disclosure laws, employment in small industries or within highly concentrated industries is disguised in an employment range rather than displayed as an absolute employment figure. Unfortunately, these data lag as much as two years. *County Business Patterns* tends to be more consistent over time than the ES data and has been published regularly since 1964, making it valuable for time series analysis.

Travis County: Descriptions of the Study Area

Travis County, which is dominated by the City of Austin, capitol of the State of Texas, lies in the geographic middle of the state's central corridor. Its 1980 population was 419,573; over 83 percent resided in the City of Austin. The racial composition of the county at that time was roughly 70.7 percent white (non-Hispanic), 10.6 percent black, and 17.2 percent Hispanic. The overall labor force participation rate was 69.3 percent in 1980, making it among the highest levels in the state. Austin has enjoyed tremendous growth since 1980, with its labor force increasing by 30.5 percent between 1980 and the third quarter, 1984. This growth has been accompanied by an unemployment rate which remained below the 4 percent mark over the period. Population growth is expected to increase to 583,699 by 1990, representing an annual growth rate of approximately 4 percent.

Industrial Structure

The Travis County economy has enjoyed the consistent growth of several industries over the study period. Total civilian nonagricultural employment was 272,954 in 1984 (first quarter), with major employment concentrations located in government (28.9 percent), services (20.1 percent), and retail trade (18.2 percent). (See table 3-1.) The government sector is comprised primarily of state government workers and educational employment. Within the services sector, business services SIC 73 and health services SIC 80 clearly predominate. From an employment standpoint, Travis County does not have a significant manufacturing sector, since area manufacturing employment comprises only 11.9 percent of total employment. This sector also shows very poor diversification, with almost 63 percent of local manufacturing in SIC 36 electric and electronic equipment, SIC 35 machinery except electrical, and SIC 27 printing and publishing (table 3-2).

In terms of business establishments, 86.5 percent of the 11,184 area businesses employ 20 or fewer workers. Moreover, 55 percent of businesses have between one and four employees. The significant deviation from this small business trend is in manufacturing where several larger establishments dominate the electronics, scientific instruments, and machinery except electrical industries (table 3-3). Notable business establishment increases are found in the finance, insurance and real estate sectors, especially in real estate, and in services, particularly in business services. Although analysis at the major division level may mask declines in specific industries, it is significant that the net number of business establishments has risen by almost 8 percent per year and that every major employment sector has shown considerable growth.

Table 3-1
Employment Structure of Travis County, Texas
First Quarter 1984

SIC (A)	Industry (B)	Civ. Non-Ag. Emp. (C)	No. of Bus. Estabs. (D)	Local % of Tot. Emp. (E)	Nat'l % of Tot. Emp. (F)	Coef. of Spec. (E/F) (G)
	Total All Industries	272,949	11,184	100.00%	100.00%	1.00
...	Agriculture, Forestry, Fishing	891	149	.33	.30	1.10*
...	Mining	615	71	.23	.92	.25
...	Contract Construction	18,915	1,535	6.93	4.23	1.64*
17	Special Trade Contractors	10,233	870	3.75	2.30	1.64*
...	Manufacturing	32,589	577	11.94	21.40	.56
20	Food and Kindred Products	1,662	31	.61	1.75	.35
22	Textile Mill	0	1	.00	.85	.00
23	Apparel	89	9	.04	1.35	.03
24	Lumber and Wood	887	43	.33	.78	.43
25	Furniture/Fixtures	1,408	18	.52	.54	.97
26	Paper/Allied Products	85	4	.04	.74	.06
27	Printing/Publishing	3,510	179	1.29	1.46	.89
28	Chemicals	1,068	19	.40	1.18	.34
29	Petroleum/Coal	44	5	.02	.21	.10
30	Rubber/Plastics	239	15	.09	.88	.11
31	Leather/Leather Products	31	3	.02	.24	.09
32	Stone, Clay, Glass	1,493	30	.55	.65	.85
33	Primary Metals	121	4	.05	.98	.06
34	Fabricated Metals	1,620	59	.60	1.62	.38
35	Machinery exc. Electric	8,585	50	3.15	2.47	1.28*
36	Electric and Electronic	8,404	48	3.08	2.43	1.27*
37	Transportation Equipment	330	11	.13	2.14	.07
38	Instruments	2,084	24	.77	.78	.99
39	Misc. Manufacturing	922	24	.34	.44	.78
...	Transportation and Utilities	7,448	287	2.73	5.13	.54
...	Wholesale Trade	11,487	693	4.21	5.91	.72
...	Retail Trade	49,523	2,151	18.15	16.79	1.09*
54	Food Stores	7,624	138	2.80	2.76	1.02*
58	Eating and Drinking	18,843	655	6.91	5.26	1.32*
...	Finance, Insurance, Real Estate	17,802	1,315	6.53	6.12	1.07*
...	Services	54,768	4,157	20.07	21.82	.92
73	Business Services	13,677	851	5.02	4.31	1.17*
80	Health Services	11,964	785	4.39	6.63	.67
89	Miscellaneous Services	6,929	457	2.54	1.23	2.07*
99	Government, Total	78,861	249	28.90	17.43	1.66*

* denotes basic industry in Travis County

Source: Texas Employment Commission, <u>Covered Wages and Employment</u>
         (ES-202), 1st Quarter 1984; Bureau of Labor Statistics, <u>Employment</u>
         <u>and Earnings</u>, March 1984

Table 3-2
Employment and Wages by Detailed Industry
Travis County, Texas
First Quarter 1984

SIC (A)	Industry (B)	No. of Bus. Estabs. (C)	Employment (D)	Total Wages (E)
07	Agriculture Services	137	843	2,468,774.08
13	Oil and Gas	67	574	4,260,015.81
15	Gen. Building Con.	548	5,869	29,757,890.03
16	Heavy Construction	117	2,812	12,207,084.98
17	Special Trade Contractors	870	10,233	44,631,860.06
20	Food and Kindred Prod.	31	1,662	6,183,787.14
23	Apparel	9	89	225,306.16
24	Lumber and Wood	43	887	4,359,910.66
25	Furniture/Fixtures	18	1,408	4,419,463.18
26	Paper/Allied Products	4	85	252,405.54
27	Printing/Publishing	179	3,510	18,014,532.25
28	Chemicals	19	1,068	5,186,061.22
29	Petroleum/Coal	5	44	416,185.12
30	Rubber/Plastics	15	239	992,910.94
32	Stone, Clay, Glass	30	1,493	7,697,198.42
34	Fabricated Metals	59	1,620	7,386,489.63
35	Machinery exc. Electric	50	8,585	62,791,606.27
36	Electric and Electronic	48	8,404	46,499,706.74
37	Transportation Equipment	11	330	1,204,433.92
38	Instruments	24	2,084	11,948,691.30
39	Misc. Manufacturing	24	922	3,132,449.38
40	Local and Interurban	12	618	2,209,845.29
42	Trucking and Warehouse	131	1,642	7,760,889.45
45	Air Transportation	20	567	3,465,597.20
46	Pipe Lines	4	25	214,754.81
47	Transportation Services	59	398	1,560,949.23
48	Communication	42	3,640	22,994,012.98
49	Electric and Gas	14	543	2,887,626.36
50	Wholesale Trade, Durable	485	8,376	53,602,698.34
51	Wholesale Trade, Nondur.	208	3,111	16,880,549.28
52	Building Materials	117	2,255	9,093,724.77
53	General Merchandise	21	5,221	11,931,401.18
54	Food Stores	138	7,624	22,011,847.95
55	Automotive Dealers	267	4,318	21,959,576.41
56	Apparel and Accessories	182	3,032	7,138,820.11
57	Furniture, Retail	202	2,148	8,488,608.44
58	Eating and Drinking	655	18,843	32,185,378.73
59	Misc. Retail	569	6,080	17,707,018.54
60	Banking	42	3,408	16,820,393.55
61	Credit Agencies	111	2,680	16,590,266.26
62	Security, Commodity	44	440	5,166,153.80
63	Insurance Carriers	111	4,349	20,894,324.75
64	Insurance Agents	235	1,681	7,472,374.15
65	Real Estate	707	4,774	19,921,590.69
70	Hotels and Lodging	91	4,026	8,874,468.06
72	Personal Services	297	3,241	8,294,278.29
73	Business Services	851	13,677	55,880,872.97
75	Auto Repair, Service Sta.	262	1,981	7,941,059.00
76	Misc. Repair	108	639	2,620,481.21
78	Motion Pictures	29	339	722,511.63
79	Amusement and Rec.	99	1,142	3,110,712.15
80	Health Services	785	11,964	57,670,682.68
81	Legal Services	364	2,528	16,222,614.66
82	Educational Services	49	1,365	3,824,097.58
83	Social Services	174	3,683	8,467,575.96
86	Membership Orgs.	320	2,776	12,512,333.81
88	Private Households	270	446	868,318.57
89	Misc. Services	457	6,926	42,011,107.95
99	Nonclassifiable Estabs.	16	50	197,535.33
	Total Private	10,951	194,092	836,024,214.11
	State Agencies	141	46,811	220,560,020.81
	Local Govt.	64	22,910	103,199,216.01
	Federal Agencies	44	9,140	43,337,612.30
	Total Govt.	249	78,861	367,096,849.12
	Total	11,200	272,954	1,203,121,063.23

Source: Texas Employment Commission

Table 3-3
Covered Employment and Business Establishments
Travis County, Texas
First Quarter 1981-1984

SIC (A)	Industry (B)	Bus. Estabs. 1981 (C)	Bus. Estabs. 1984 (D)	Absolute and % Change in Bus. Estabs. 1981–84 (E) (F)		% Bus. Estabs. with 20 or Fewer Emps. (G)
	Total All Industries	9,114	11,184	2,070	22.7%	86.5%
...	Agriculture, Forestry, Fishing	109	149	40	36.7	97.0
...	Mining	44	71	27	61.4	91.7
...	Contract Construction	1,187	1,535	348	29.3	85.5
17	Special Trade Contractors	734	870	136	18.5	86.4
...	Manufacturing	474	577	103	21.7	69.1
20	Food and Kindred Products	27	31	4	14.8	44.0
22	Textile Mill	1	1	0	0.0	50.0
23	Apparel	5	9	4	80.0	77.8
24	Lumber and Wood	36	43	7	19.4	59.1
25	Furniture/Fixtures	17	18	1	5.9	63.6
26	Paper/Allied Products	2	4	2	100.0	100.0
27	Printing/Publishing	144	179	35	24.3	79.8
28	Chemicals	13	19	6	46.2	64.3
29	Petroleum/Coal	2	5	3	150.0	100.0
30	Rubber/Plastics	16	15	-1	-6.3	77.8
31	Leather/Leather Products	4	3	-1	-25.0	100.0
32	Stone, Clay, Glass	27	30	3	11.1	60.0
33	Primary Metals	4	4	0	0.0	33.3
34	Fabricated Metals	46	59	13	28.3	67.7
35	Machinery exc. Electric	45	50	5	11.1	66.7
36	Electric and Electronic	35	48	13	37.1	60.0
37	Transportation Equipment	9	11	2	22.2	62.5
38	Instruments	20	24	4	20.0	56.0
39	Misc. Manufacturing	21	24	3	14.3	87.1
...	Transportation and Utilities	229	287	58	25.3	71.5
...	Wholesale Trade	592	693	101	17.1	85.5
...	Retail Trade	1,913	2,151	238	12.4	83.2
54	Food Stores	124	138	14	11.3	81.2
58	Eating and Drinking	572	655	83	14.5	69.1
...	Finance, Insurance, Real Estate	996	1,315	319	32.0	86.2
...	Services	3,329	4,157	828	24.9	89.8
73	Business Services	538	851	313	58.2	84.4
80	Health Services	649	785	136	21.0	91.4
89	Miscellaneous Services	319	457	138	43.3	100.0
99	Government, Total	241	249	8	3.3	---

Source: Texas Employment Commission, Covered Wages and Employment (ES-202), 1st Quarter 1984.
Department of Commerce, County Business Patterns, 1982.

Firm Size

The significance of identifying the employment structure of firms in an industry is exemplified in the strategies incorporated in direct employer contact situations. Depending on an agency's previous success rates with either small or large firms, the approach for job placement or securing on-the-job (OJT) training contracts from a private employer will vary from small to large companies. Smaller firms tend not to develop a large degree of in-house training capability and may, therefore, be more receptive to outside training proposals. Many smaller firms are locally owned, prompting them to be community-oriented and willing to help disadvantaged workers within the community. Smaller firms, however, have significantly lower potential job volume than larger firms. Large firms tend to have expanded in-house training capabilities and stronger internal promotion policies resulting in fewer job openings aside from entry level positions. The positive aspect of dealing with large firms is the greater number of potential total job openings which occur through growth and, especially, labor turnover. Although the success rate of generating employment and training-related contracts may be lower with large firms, fewer positive contacts are necessary to achieve a greater volume of job opportunities.

Economic Base Analysis

The final element in recognizing the underpinnings of the local industrial economy is identifying the economic base. *Basic* (export) industries are those that generate greater amounts of income and employment than is necessary to meet the community's own consumption needs. The rule of thumb for identifying a basic industry is whether the local area receives income from outside the area from sales of a particular good or service. *External* (export) income translates into additional units of local employment to produce the goods or services which generate income from outside the area. Using this definition, the economic base of an area does not have to be natural resource- or manufacturing-based. Indeed, areas which serve as regional finance and retail centers clearly export these services and are reliant upon these industries as sources of external income and employment generation. Industries which are not classified as basic are termed *service* or import industries. These industries generally are population-serving or ancillary manufacturing, and do not produce enough goods or services to export from the area. In some cases the local area must import large amounts of these goods or services to meet local consumption needs.

These relationships can be measured using *coefficients of specialization.* The algebraic construct of the coefficient of specialization is specified in terms of an industry's specialization within the local economy in relation to that industry's national concentration in the total U.S. economy. Where the local industry has a greater concentration of total local employment than the industry has on a national basis, the industry is termed an export industry in the local area. If a local industry has a coefficient of specialization greater than 1, it is considered a basic industry. (Appendix 4 covers in greater detail the concepts of economic base analysis.)

Travis County has several basic industries; the most significant is government. As previously observed with the employment and business establishment data, the coefficients of specialization indicate concentrations in machinery except electrical, electric and electronic equipment, retail trade, contract construction, business services, and real estate. Also consistent with the employment data, the lack of concentration in manufacturing and heavy dependence upon services and the public sector make Travis County a poorly diversified area. The area is at least partially sheltered against business cycle downturns, however, because of the large government payrolls and large trade sectors.

Step 2
Historical Trend in Industry Employment

The second step in industrial analysis is to assess recent historical trends in the local economy. In order to evaluate future performance in terms of job opportunity, it is helpful to identify industry growth or decline over a recent historical period.

Selection of Base and Terminal Years

Before one can analyze historical trend, it is necessary to specify the time period under consideration. Because most economies (national or local) tend to fluctuate over time, with periods of prosperity and periods of decline, it is essential to select two years which best represent the *overall* performance of the local economy as the base and terminal years for analysis. Without such care, the analyst could possibly pick two years, one of which was a boom period and one a recession year, which misrepresent the overall economic trend. As historical trends can often serve as indicators of future performance, to misspecify the historical trend would remove a great deal of the associated predictive power.

There are several ways to select the base and terminal years for trend analysis. The easiest method would be to graph 10 to 15 years of total employment data against time. Connecting the points gives an indication of the prosperity and decline which have been the historical economic pattern over the period. Having plotted this total employment series, the practitioner may then draw a straight line through the scatterplot of points which provides a general direction of trend. Where 10 or more years of data have been plotted, the analyst must consider the possibility of two or more distinct trends having taken place over the period. After the trend line has been drawn, the two points which fall closest to the line should be selected as the base and terminal years. It is recommended that the terminal year be as recent as possible to reflect current conditions in relation to historical trends.

It should be mentioned that this technique of "eyeballing" the scatterplot to determine trend is a crude measure. A much more sophisticated technique is the use of simple linear regression analysis to determine a line of best fit to the scatterplot of data. Using time as the independent variable and the total industry employment as the dependent variable, employment data for the past 10 to 15 years should be entered. The regression equation will compute the slope and Y intercept (constant term) from which to draw a straight line of best fit (industry trend line).

Fitting the industry trend line to the scatterplot of industry employment data for the various years illustrates that the trend line will fall closer to actual employment levels in some years and further away in others. The years which fall closest to the best fit line are most representative of the overall (linear) trend in industry employment. The final selection of the base and terminal years should be limited to those years which most closely resemble the overall long-run trend in industry employment and should be no more than five or six years apart. If the base and terminal years are too far apart, it is possible that two or more distinct economic cycles could be included and not be identified as such.

Issues

Having selected the base and terminal years for analysis, it is again important to delineate the specific information that is to be gleaned from historical trend analysis. Some of the issues to be addressed at this stage would include:

(1) What has been the trend in total industry employment over the past 12-15 years?
(2) What two years are the most representative of that trend?
(3) What was industry employment in the base year?
(4) What was industry employment in the terminal year?
(5) Which industries were the largest employers in the base year?
(6) Which industries are the largest in the terminal year (in terms of employment)?

(7) Which industries have experienced the greatest *percentage* increase in employment between the base and terminal years?

(8) Which industries have experienced the greatest *absolute* increase in employment between the base and the terminal years?

(9) How has the employment change in each industry been affected by national, local, and overall industry forces?

Table 3-4 displays Travis County industry employment levels for 1980 to 1984 and the change between 1981 and 1984. The years 1981 and 1984 were selected for trend years because they fell closest to the trend line drawn through the scatterplot of total industry employment from 1974 through 1984 (chart 3-1). Although the year 1983 on an annualized basis actually falls slightly closer than 1984 to the trend line, second and third quarter 1984 employment figures indicate that first quarter 1985 will be another very high data point, which will pull the trend line closer to the 1984 annual figure.

Between 1981 and 1984, total employment rose from 221,656 to 272,949, representing a growth of 51,293 net new jobs (a 23.1 percent growth rate). The industries experiencing the greatest absolute increases were services, especially business services; retail trade, noticeably eating and drinking establishments; electric and electronic manufacturing SIC 36; and contract construction. The only major decline was in the machinery except electrical industry SIC 35, which reached a peak of 9,926 in 1981, and fell to an employment level of 8,585 by 1984. The largest percentage increases came in contract construction, which experienced explosive growth between 1983 and 1984; business services; and electric and electronic equipment. Lumber and wood products, although a relatively small industry, experienced large percentage increases during the study period, as did fabricated metals, eating and drinking places, and miscellaneous services.

Table 3-4
Recent Historical Trends in Industrial Employment
Travis County, Texas
First Quarter 1980-1984

SIC (A)	Industry (B)	1980 (C)	1981 (D)	1982 (E)	1983 (F)	1984 (G)
	Total All Industries	208,220	221,656	232,344	244,333	272,949
...	Agriculture, Forestry, Fishing	542	625	627	781	891
...	Mining	192	342	411	501	615
...	Contract Construction	11,789	12,269	12,204	13,685	18,915
17	Special Trade Contractors	6,235	6,754	6,835	7,956	10,233
...	Manufacturing	25,138	27,380	27,948	28,005	32,589
20	Food and Kindred Products	1,564	1,437	1,611	1,592	1,662
22	Textile Mill	0	49	57	34	0
23	Apparel	56	31	38	65	89
24	Lumber and Wood	424	500	526	660	887
25	Furniture/Fixtures	1,058	1,118	1,303	1,344	1,408
26	Paper/Allied Products	49	44	27	30	85
27	Printing/Publishing	2,695	2,908	2,975	3,078	3,510
28	Chemicals	360	367	394	373	1,068
29	Petroleum/Coal	32	32	39	42	44
30	Rubber/Plastics	347	387	302	220	239
31	Leather/Leather Products	49	51	56	58	31
32	Stone, Clay, Glass	1,112	1,108	1,198	1,395	1,493
33	Primary Metals	56	60	151	125	121
34	Fabricated Metals	1,019	1,112	1,450	1,495	1,620
35	Machinery exc. Electric	8,742	9,926	9,174	8,414	8,585
36	Electric and Electronic	4,601	5,154	5,388	6,263	8,404
37	Transportation Equipment	687	482	480	236	330
38	Instruments	1,559	1,908	1,999	1,840	2,084
39	Misc. Manufacturing	728	706	772	736	922
...	Transportation and Utilities	6,054	6345	7,165	6,750	7,448
...	Wholesale Trade	7,634	7,743	9,397	11,519	11,487
...	Retail Trade	37,169	37,832	42,919	44,120	49,523
54	Food Stores	5,897	5,572	6,031	6,738	7,624
58	Eating and Drinking	13,070	13,582	15,597	16,639	18,843
...	Finance, Insurance, Real Estate	12,095	13,359	14,192	15,770	17,802
...	Services	35,103	40,626	43,288	45,853	54,768
73	Business Services	8,543	9,131	11,325	11,365	13,677
80	Health Services	7,466	11,273	9,475	10,172	11,964
89	Miscellaneous Services	2,507	2,846	3,079	3,987	6,929
99	Government, Total	72,504	75,135	74,193	77,349	78,861

Source: Texas Employment Commission, <u>Covered Wages and Employment</u> (ES-202), 1st Quarter 1980-1984.

Chart 3-1
Changes in Industrial Employment
Travis County, Texas
1974-1984

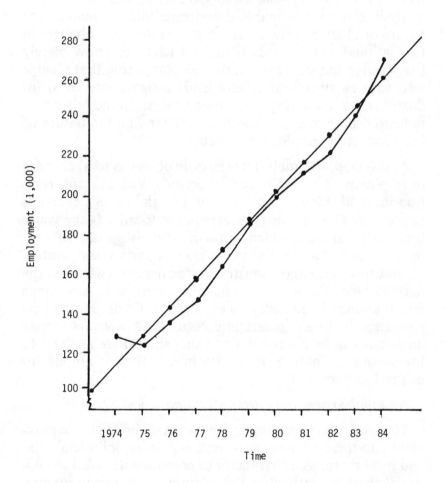

Although the Travis County economy is showing signs of diversifying its base through expansion of the manufacturing sector (especially in electronics), the area is still driven by public sector expenditures and relies on population-serving smaller business for the majority of its employment growth.

Shift-Share Analysis

In order to better analyze the county's economic base, a technique called *shift-share analysis* may be used. Shift-share analysis can be a valuable descriptive tool to analyze the nature of change in the local economy relative to changes in the national economy. It is not sufficient to know merely that change has occurred; rather, decomposing that change into various structural effects lends insights into local industry shifts. Including shift-share analysis in the process of industrial base analysis aids in understanding the nature of local industrial employment changes.

At this step, the analyst has already observed total changes in employment over a historical period. With that information in mind, identifying the nature of the change becomes important. If an industry is expanding locally, is the cause total national employment growth ("a rising tide lifts all boats"), or is it a result of increased demand for the product so that this particular industry is growing everywhere in the nation? Does the local area have a comparative advantage which allows the industry to expand locally despite its performance in other geographic regions? Answers to these questions can be approximated using shift-share analysis to investigate the nature of change in a region or among industrial sectors.

National Share, Industrial Mix, and Local Share

The shift-share technique divides total change in employment into three components—national share, industrial mix, and local share. The first factor or component, called the *national share,* is defined as the amount of change in an area that is attributable to the change in a larger area of which it is a part, namely the state or the nation. This factor describes the change that would be expected simply by virtue of the area being a part of a changing whole, other factors held constant. Specifically, if the nation as a whole is growing, one would expect that national growth would exert a positive influence on growth of the local area.

The second factor or component is called the *industrial mix*. This indicates the portion of change that is attributable to the change in the industry being analyzed. We know that a given industry may be expanding or contracting more rapidly or slowly than other industries or the nation as a whole; the growth rate of the nation is simply the weighted average growth of all industries. Thus the second factor is the change in a local industry that would be attributable to the growth or decline of the industry nationally, other factors held constant.

The third factor is called the regional or *local share*. It describes the extent to which factors unique to the local area have caused a growth or decline in local employment of an industrial group. We know that even in periods of prosperity some communities grow faster than others. The local component aids in identifying a local area's economic strength. Those industrial sectors with *positive local share* components offer the greatest potential for job opportunity (holding all other factors equal) since they are increasing at rates greater than the national industry performance. The caveat here, of course, is that if an industry is *declining* nationally, the local industry could still show a positive local share effect if it were declining at a slower rate than the industry nationally. The ideal situation, then, is to identify those industries with both a positive industry mix effect *and* a positive local share. Although shift-share analysis cannot explain the *causes* of each component, the three components analyzed in tandem can provide great deal of evidence about the national effects on local industry performance. Only an analyst with a complete understanding of the local economic environment is equipped to pinpoint the determinants of local industry employment changes.

Methodology for Estimating Shift-Share

Shift-Share Step 1

To compute the National Share Estimate for a local industry, multiply the employment level in the *local* industry in the base year *times* the percent change in overall *U.S.* employment.

Example: 9,131 (business services, Travis County 1981)
            x.0219 (Percent change, U.S. total employment,
            _____ 1981-1984)

            = 200 *National Share Estimate*

Interpretation: Between 1981-1984, employment in the business services industry in Travis County grew by 4,546 employees. If it had expanded at an "average" rate of growth, employment in that industry in Travis County would have grown by 200 employees, thus, employment growth in that industry in Travis County was far above "average."

Why was growth above average? Was growth in business services above average throughout the U.S.?

Shift-Share Step 2

To compute the Industrial Mix Estimate for a local industry, first subtract the percent change in total U.S. employment between the base and terminal year from the percent change in the industry's national employment over the period. Then, multiply this "Industrial Mix Rate" times *local* employment in that industry in the base year.

Example: .2680 (Percent change in employment, U.S.
                    business services, 1981-1984)
           -.0219 (Percent change in total employment,
            _____ U.S. 1981-1984)

            .2461 (Industrial Mix Rate)
           x9,131 (Employment, Travis County
            _____ business services, 1981)

            = 2,247 *Industrial Mix Estimate*

Interpretation: Between 1981-1984, employment in the business services industry throughout the U.S. grew above "average." If employment in Travis County had expanded at the U.S. industry rate, 2,447 employees would have been added. Of those employees, 200 could be attributed to growth at the same rate as the nation on the whole and 2,247 of them due to growth in the business services industry throughout the U.S. Because total industry employment in Travis County grew by 4,546 employees, it can be said that the local area experienced growth at a rate above the national industry average.

Is the above average growth in business services in Travis County attributable to factors peculiar and unique to Travis County?

Shift Share Step 3

To compute the Local Share Estimate for a local industry, first subtract the percent change in the industry's *national* employment between the base and terminal years from the percent change in *local* employment in the industry, then *multiply* this "Local Share Rate" *times* the *local* employment in that industry in the base year.

Example: .4980   (Percent change in employment, Travis County business services, 1981-1984)

        -.2680   (Percent change in employment, U.S. business services, 1981-1984)

        _____

        .2300   (Local Share Rate)
        x9,131 (Employment, Travis County business services, 1981)

        _____

        = 2,100 *Local Share Estimate*

Interpretation: Between 1981 and 1984, employment in business services in Travis County grew at a rate above the "average" rate of growth for that industry in other areas of the U.S. If business services in Travis County had expanded at the U.S. average rate, employment would have expanded by 2,447 persons. However, the actual employment growth was 4,546. That is, some factor has affected the industry's employment growth in Travis County that has resulted in an above average growth rate in the local area. The result is a very large comparative advantage in Travis County which allows local growth in business services to outstrip the growth of the industry nationwide and outpace overall national growth. Shift-share analysis cannot assist the practitioner in identifying the local factors that influenced this growth, but it does pinpoint sectors in the local economy which enjoy some comparative advantage. Conversely, where negative local share components accompany positive industrial mix estimates, the practitioner may want to investigate why that industry performed better nationwide than in the local area.

Results for Travis County

Table 3-5 displays shift-share results for Travis County. Not surprising, given the overall growth in the county, all major divisions of the Travis County economy had positive local share components. Large *negative* local shares were found in health services, machinery except electrical, transportation equipment and rubber and plastics. The most noticeable *positive* local share was in government, with a very large local share despite a very large negative industrial mix. Positive local shares were also found in manufacturing (especially the electronics industry), both wholesale and retail trade sectors, and contract construction. It is evident from the shift-share coefficients that, with few exceptions, the overall economic growth in Travis County has carried nationally stagnant industries to prosperity in the local area. Shift-share analysis reveals a very healthy local economy in all major sectors and one which far outperformed the national economy in most sectors.

Table 3-5
Shift-Share Analysis
Travis County, Texas
1981-1984

SIC (A)	Industry (B)	Absolute Change 1981-1984 (C)	National Share (D)	Industrial Mix (E)	Local Share (F)
	Total All Industries	51,293	4,855	-3,325	49,763
...	Agriculture, Forestry, Fishing	266	14	---	---
...	Mining	273	8	-33	298
...	Contract Construction	6,646	269	-491	6,868
17	Special Trade Contractors	3,479	148	-621	3,952
...	Manufacturing	5,209	600	-1,807	6,416
20	Food and Kindred Products	225	31	-70	264
22	Textile Mill	-47	1	-6	-42
23	Apparel	58	1	-2	59
24	Lumber and Wood	387	11	17	359
25	Furniture/Fixtures	290	24	-1	267
26	Paper/Allied Products	41	1	-2	42
27	Printing/Publishing	602	64	23	515
28	Chemicals	701	8	-22	715
29	Petroleum/Coal	12	1	-4	15
30	Rubber/Plastics	-149	8	36	-193
31	Leather/Leather Products	-19	1	-6	-14
32	Stone, Clay, Glass	385	24	-114	475
33	Primary Metals	61	1	-14	74
34	Fabricated Metals	508	24	-115	599
35	Machinery exc. Electric	-1,340	217	-1,250	-307
36	Electric and Electronic	3,251	113	29	3,109
37	Transportation Equipment	-151	11	6	-168
38	Instruments	176	42	-27	161
39	Misc. Manufacturing	216	15	-32	233
...	Transportation and Utilities	1,103	139	-311	1,275
...	Wholesale Trade	3,744	170	-248	3,822
...	Retail Trade	11,691	829	-189	11,051
54	Food Stores	2,052	122	18	1,912
58	Eating and Drinking	5,261	297	-129	5,093
...	Finance, Insurance, Real Estate	4,443	293	-174	4,324
...	Services	14,142	890	2,438	10,814
73	Business Services	4,546	200	2,247	2,100
80	Health Services	691	246	1,103	-659
89	Miscellaneous Services	4,080	62	166	3,852
99	Government, Total	3,726	1,646	-2,705	4,785

Source: Texas Employment Commission, Covered Wages and Employment
(ES-202), 1981 and 1984.
Bureau of Labor Statistics, Employment and Earnings, March 1984.

Step 3
Industry Employment Projections

Following examination of (1) the current industrial structure and (2) recent and historical trends by industry, the
study of industry employment projections completes the
analysis of the local industrial structure. Industry projections provide employment data, by industry categories, for a
base year, current estimated year, and target year, so that it
is possible to calculate absolute and percentage growth
(decline) over these periods. Employment projections are
valuable in identifying those industries which are expected to
grow, decline, or remain stable in employment over a future
time period.

Issues

Some of the questions to be answered regarding future industry employment levels are the following:

(1) How many total job opportunities are projected to
    occur by the terminal year of the projections?
(2) Does this represent a growth or decline in total in-
    dustry employment?
(3) Which industries are projected to have the greatest
    number of jobs due to growth and due to replace-
    ment?
(4) What is the net addition/decline of jobs in each in-
    dustry over the projected period?
(5) Which industries are expected to gain the greatest
    number of additional jobs?
(6) Which industries have the highest projected *growth
    rate* over the projection period?
(7) Which industries expect to gain the greatest number
    of jobs due to growth and due to replacement?

Data Sources

The most complete data source for industry employment projections is the Bureau of Labor Statistics' Occupational Employment Statistics (OES) program. The OES program consists of three separate components. One of these, the OES projections series, is a count of industry employment, based on a sample survey, projected forward to a target year. These projections are available in most states at the statewide level and for many major MSAs across the country.

There is no existing national data program which provides detailed industrial projections at the county level. If the county is part of an existing MSA, OES projections for the MSA are used to determine future employment opportunities within the entire labor market. Industry employment projections are also available from the Bureau of Economic Analysis (BEA) for states and metropolitan areas. Various universities are also sources for such projections.

This monograph does not cover the development of local area employment projections for industry sectors. There are several methodologies available for performing such projections, including the use of industry-specific regression models, moving average forecasting techniques such as Box-Jenkins, shift-share models, and national census-share techniques. It is recommended that the practitioner make best use of projections calculated by professional groups, since properly specified and accurate local area projections are difficult to develop. In the volatile economic climate of the 1980s, industry employment projections are likely to be imprecise at best. They are probably most useful in a relative sense, whereby the analyst can determine that one industry is expected to grow at a faster or slower rate than another, given a set of predetermined assumptions.

Employment Projections for Travis County

Travis County, and especially the City of Austin, represents an integral part of the Austin metropolitan statistical area (MSA). As such, industry projections for the MSA represent trends which also reflect the nature of Travis County labor conditions. Table 3-6 presents industry employment projections for the Austin MSA. Employment was projected to increase by 38 percent over the 7-year

Table 3-6
Industry Employment Projections to 1985
Austin MSA, Texas

SIC (A)	Industry (B)	1978 Avg. Annual Empl. (C)	1985 Avg. Annual Empl. (D)	Absolute Change 1978-85 (E)	Percent Change 1978-85 (F)	Annual Avg. Openings (G)
	Total All Industries	215,650	296,700	81,050	38	11,578
...	Mining	550	1,050	500	91	71
...	Contract Construction	13,400	18,050	4,650	35	664
17	Special Trade Contractors	6,500	8,600	2,100	32	300
...	Manufacturing	25,600	44,850	19,250	75	2,750
20	Food and Kindred Products	1,700	2,050	350	21	50
22	Textile Mill	550	650	100	18	14
24	Lumber and Wood	500	750	250	50	36
25	Furniture/Fixtures	1,850	1,650	-200	-11	-35
27	Printing/Publishing	2,600	3,600	1,000	38	143
28	Chemicals	450	2,450	2,000	444	286
30	Rubber/Plastics	350	450	100	29	14
32	Stone, Clay, Glass	1,200	1,750	500	46	71
33	Primary Metals	200	350	150	75	21
34	Fabricated Metals	1,000	1,650	650	65	93
35	Machinery exc. Electric	6,350	11,050	4,700	74	671
36	Electric and Electronic	5,150	12,800	7,650	149	1,093
37	Transportation Equipment	1,000	1,600	600	60	86
38	Instruments	1,700	2,750	1,050	62	150
39	Misc. Manufacturing	750	1,000	250	33	36
...	Transportation and Utilities	10,150	13,450	3,300	33	471
...	Wholesale Trade	7,100	10,650	3,550	50	507
...	Retail Trade	38,700	53,850	15,150	39	2,164
54	Food Stores	6,000	8,650	2,650	44	378
58	Eating and Drinking	13,250	19,000	5,750	43	821
...	Finance, Insurance, Real Estate	12,900	18,150	5,250	41	750
...	Services	75,100	100,000	24,900	33	3,557
73	Business Services	6,500	12,250	5,750	88	821
80	Health Services	11,000	15,650	4,650	42	664
89	Miscellaneous Services	2,150	3,250	1,100	51	157

Source: Texas Employment Commission, Area Occupational Demand Forecast 1985.

period from 1978 to 1985. This translates to over 81,000 net new jobs over the period, with an average of 5.3 percent or 11,578 net new jobs per year. The greatest number of new jobs was expected to occur in services, retail trade, and the electronics industry. On a percentage basis, chemicals, electronics, business services, and mining were projected to show the greatest gains.

In addition to local area projections, state and national employment projections can be examined to identify the industries expected to experience the greatest growth or decline for their respective regions. To illustrate the imprecise nature of these estimates, it is interesting to compare 1985 industry employment projections to the *actual* Travis County industry employment in the first quarter of 1984. From table 3-1, it is apparent that the 1984 employment levels of the following industries had already exceeded their 1985 projections: contract construction, special trade contractors SIC 17, lumber and wood SIC 24, wholesale trade, business services SIC 73, and miscellaneous services SIC 89.

Step 4
Current Employment Trends

The fourth step in the analytical process is to identify the most current economic trends within the local area. With assessments already completed for the historical and future periods, the current economic situation can be researched from a more enlightened perspective. Analysis of the current employment situation can be divided into five subgroups: (1) recent employment trends, (2) average weekly hours and earnings, (3) labor turnover and replacement needs, (4) current job openings, and (5) mass layoffs or plant closings.

Issues

As with the previous analytical steps, several questions should be considered while reviewing the data. Such questions include:

(1) What changes have occurred in the civilian labor force over the past month and year?

(2) What has been the net change in the number of unemployed persons?

(3) What has been the net change in the number of employed persons?

(4) Which industries have experienced *increases* in employment?

(5) Which industries have experienced *decreases* in employment?

(6) Which industries show increases in average weekly hours worked?

(7) Are the industries that reflect declining employment also evidencing decreases in average weekly hours of work?

(8) Which industries have the highest weekly earnings? Which the lowest?

(9) Which industries have the highest and lowest quarterly new hire rates?

(10) Which industries have the greatest number of potential new hires (based on the combination of current employment and new hire rate)?

(11) Which industries have the greatest number of available job openings filed with the ES?

(12) How many job openings have remained unfilled for 20 days or more?

(13) Have there been any mass layoffs or plant closings which might have an effect on the number of unemployed?

Data Sources

The monthly *Labor Market Information Newsletter,* published by the Research and Statistics units of the ES, is a depository of local data from which the research on current local economic conditions may commence. Industry employment data published in the *Newsletter* are collected through a federal-state cooperative statistical program, the Current Employment Statistics (CES) program (also referred to as BLS-790, named after the Bureau of Labor Statistics form number which is sent to employers as part of the sample survey). Although these data lack the detail and coverage of *County Business Patterns* and ES-202 data, they are available with only a one-month time lag for every state and MSA in the country. Also included in the *Newsletter* are current statistics on hours and earnings and other economic developments over the past month.

Tables 3-7 and 3-8 display sample CES data for the Austin MSA and the State of Texas, respectively, published from the Texas monthly newsletter. Consistent with the recent historical pattern of sizable growth, the Austin MSA added 13,300 total new jobs between March 1983 and March 1984. Every major division except transportation and utilities exhibited growth over the period with construction and government representing over 42 percent of total growth.

Table 3-7
Current Trends in Industry Employment
Austin MSA, Texas

Industry	March 1984 <1>	Feb. 1984 <1>	March 1983 <2>
TOTAL	296,400	294,700	283,100
Manufacturing	34,400	34,500	32,800
Mining	800	800	800
Construction	19,100	18,600	16,600
Transportation, Communication, Utilities	8,000	8,100	8,100
Trade	66,800	66,300	63,200
Finance, Insurance, Real Estate	18,700	18,600	18,200
Services & Miscellaneous	58,800	58,800	56,700
Government	89,800	89,000	86,700

<1> Preliminary--subject to revision.
<2> Revised.

Source: Texas Employment Commission, Texas Labor Market Newsletter, April 1984.

Table 3-8
Current Employment in the State of Texas (1)

Industry	March 1984 <2>	Feb. 1984 <3>	March 1983 <3>	Change From Feb. 1984	Change From Mar. 1983
TOTAL NONAGRICULTURAL EMPLOYMENT <4>	6,287,000	6,262,600	6,127,000	24,400	160,000
Manufacturing	979,100	972,300	957,800	6,800	21,300
Durable Goods	563,900	557,700	550,000	6,200	13,900
Lumber, Wood Products	41,000	40,600	37,900	400	3,100
Logging Camps, Mills	7,500	7,600	7,200	-100	300
Furniture, Fixtures	17,900	17,800	15,800	100	2,100
Stone, Clay, Glass Products	48,000	47,800	43,900	200	4,100
Concrete, Gypsum, Plaster Products	22,700	22,200	20,300	500	2,400
Primary Metal Industries	34,800	34,300	33,600	500	1,200
Fabricated Metal Products	80,500	79,900	79,700	600	800
Fabricated Structural Metal	43,500	43,400	42,700	100	800
Machinery, except Electrical	132,800	130,100	135,700	2,700	-2,900
Oil Field Machinery	43,200	41,700	46,700	1,500	-3,500
Electric, Electronic Equipment	100,100	99,300	97,000	800	3,100
Transportation Equipment	73,500	72,800	71,100	700	2,400
Aircraft, Parts	37,200	37,200	38,100	0	-900
Instruments, Related Products	23,000	22,800	22,900	200	100
Miscellaneous Manufacturing	12,300	12,300	12,400	0	-100
Nondurable Goods	415,200	414,600	407,800	600	7,400
Food, Kindred Products	95,300	96,400	92,800	-1,100	2,500
Meat Products	24,200	24,100	24,500	100	-300
Dairy Products	4,900	4,900	4,900	0	0
Bakery Products	12,500	12,400	10,600	100	1,900
Malt Beverages	3,300	3,300	3,300	0	0
Textile Mill Products	5,000	4,900	5,000	100	0
Apparel, Other Finished Textiles	62,200	61,000	60,000	1,200	2,200
Paper, Allied Products	22,100	22,200	21,500	-100	600
Printing, Publishing	70,700	70,600	68,000	100	2,700
Newspapers, Books, Misc. Publ.	35,300	35,500	35,100	-200	200
Chemicals, Allied Products	76,300	76,300	77,900	0	-1,600
Petroleum, Coal Products	42,900	42,900	44,000	0	-1,100
Petroleum Refining	39,600	39,600	40,900	0	-1,300
Leather, Leather Products	8,300	8,300	8,900	0	-600
Other Nondurable Goods	32,400	32,000	29,700	400	2,700

<1> Estimated number of nonagricultural jobs in Texas without reference to place of residence of workers.
<2> Preliminary—subject to revision.
<3> Revised.
<4> Estimated in cooperation with the Bureau of Labor Statistics and Employment & Training Administration, U.S. Department of Labor.

Source: Texas Employment Commission, Texas Labor Market Newsletter, April 1984.

Hours and Earnings

The second phase of current employment analysis is the investigation of average weekly earnings and hours worked. Average weekly hours data, in particular, assist the analyst in understanding changing production levels of industry, since a movement in weekly hours is commonly recognized as a leading indicator of the cyclical growth or decline of an industry. Because certain industrial employees traditionally do not work the standard 40 hour workweek, hours should be monitored over time to identify intraindustry trends. Knowledge of interindustry trends may only be useful in a comparative labor market analysis, or when researching industrial linkages. These data are also generally available from the monthly *Newsletter.*

Turnover

Labor turnover is an essential part of monitoring current economic conditions. Labor turnover refers to the movement into and out of jobs due to new hiring activity, layoffs, recalls or quits. As pointed out previously, new hire activity represents the biggest part of total accessions. The new hire rate is calculated as the number of newly hired workers for each 100 employed workers and can be used to forecast the number of potential job openings an industry may have over a given period. Several states calculate state-specific *industry* new hire rates by participating in the Employment Service Potential (ESP) project. This program identifies new hires by searching ES employer tax files to find new social security numbers, thus identifying changes in employment patterns. Because these data represent actual counts of accessions and separations within employer tax files, they are considered very reliable. Where state-specific new hire data are not available, national new hire rates by industry are published by the BLS and through a 1 percent social security sample survey conducted by the University of Michigan.

Potential new hires are calculated as follows:

Potential new hires = new hire rate X local employment.

For example, in calculating the number of potential new hires in Travis County for SIC 73 business services using Texas-specific quarterly new hire rates, the equation would be:

$$(SIC\ 73)\ 41.9\%\ X\ 13,677 = 5,731.$$

The 5,731 figure represents the number of job openings that are expected to become available in SIC 73 in Travis County through replacement demand in a given calendar quarter. Although many of these job openings are not formally identified through mechanisms external to the specific employer, a count of potential new hires is still a rough estimate of available future jobs. Even in periods where net growth is not occurring, there will usually continue to be hiring activity due to employee separations (for more in-depth discussion of labor turnover see appendix 1).

Table 3-9 displays potential new hires for Travis County. The Texas economy can expect replacement demand for all industries to run approximately 21.7 percent per quarter or 86.8 percent per year. New hire rates for manufacturing, government, and transportation/public utilities tend to be much lower than those in construction, retail trade and services. This is not surprising, given the number of low wage, low skill occupations which dominate the latter group. Also not surprising is that the larger industries tend also to have the largest numbers of potential new hires. However, there are numerous situations, like the comparison of manufacturing and construction, where both have a similar level of potential new hires despite the fact that the manufacturing sector has over 3 times more employment. For better understanding of labor turnover within industries, the analyst must determine the occupational structure and examine occupational separation rates within an industry.

Job Listings at the Public Employment Service

One important element of current industry trends is the number of job listings filed with the ES. Although the number of openings filed with the ES is a small percentage of total industry job vacancies, data reflecting the characteristics of listings serve several research purposes. Primarily, they are a timely source of information on available job openings. They also can be monitored over a

Table 3-9
Potential New Hires by Industry
Travis County, Texas
First Quarter 1984

SIC (A)	Industry (B)	Quarterly New Hire Rate (per 100) (C)	Local Employment 1984 (D)	Potential New Hires (E)
	Total All Industries	21.7	272,949	59,230
...	Agriculture, Forestry, Fishing	54.2	891	483
...	Mining	15.6	615	96
...	Contract Construction	39.4	18,915	7,453
17	Special Trade Contractors	39.8	10,233	4,073
...	Manufacturing	12.4	32,589	4,042
20	Food and Kindred Products	15.6	1,662	260
22	Textile Mill	11.5	0	0
23	Apparel	16.3	89	15
24	Lumber and Wood	27.2	887	242
25	Furniture/Fixtures	20.6	1,408	291
26	Paper/Allied Products	10.1	85	9
27	Printing/Publishing	17.5	3,510	615
28	Chemicals	4.5	1,068	49
29	Petroleum/Coal	3.5	44	2
30	Rubber/Plastics	17.6	239	43
31	Leather/Leather Products	12.6	31	4
32	Stone, Clay, Glass	18.3	1,493	274
33	Primary Metals	9.6	121	12
34	Fabricated Metals	17.1	1,620	278
35	Machinery exc. Electric	8.5	8,585	730
36	Electric and Electronic	8.9	8,404	748
37	Transportation Equipment	7.1	330	24
38	Instruments	8.8	2,084	184
39	Misc. Manufacturing	13.6	922	126
...	Transportation and Utilities	13.1	7,448	976
...	Wholesale Trade	14.6	11,487	1,678
...	Retail Trade	30.0	49,523	14,857
54	Food Stores	24.9	7,624	1,899
58	Eating and Drinking	45.1	18,843	8,499
...	Finance, Insurance, Real Estate	16.2	17,802	2,884
...	Services	21.6	54,768	11,830
73	Business Services	41.6	13,677	5,690
80	Health Services	19.3	11,964	2,310
89	Miscellaneous Services	14.6	6,929	1,012
99	Government, Total	8.7	78,861	6,861

Source: Texas Employment Commission, Labor Turnover Activity, Texas, 2nd
Quarter 1983; Covered Wages and Employment (ES-202), 1st Quarter 1984.

period of time and used as a cyclical indicator which rises or falls as the labor market tightens or slackens. In addition, these data have been used to identify structural imbalances existing in a given labor market.

For several years, job vacancy data systems have been challenged by critics who question their usefulness versus inherent survey problems and costs. Recently, two of the most useful data programs for reporting job openings by industry and by occupation have been cancelled due to funding cutbacks (JOB-FLO and LMI-Analytical Table Series). Identification of job order activity through the ES can still be monitored using the Employment Service Automated Reporting System (ESARS). This system is a federally-structured internal reporting system for the ES and therefore is consistent in every state. ESARS tables 7A, 7B, and 12 may be used for this purpose. Nationally, the *Occupations in Demand* monthly publication lists hard-to-fill job openings by occupation for areas throughout the nation and is available from the Employment and Training Administration (ETA/DOL) regional offices as well as from many ES agencies.

Table 3-10 displays current job openings by industry in Travis County, as reported in ESARS table 12. Most significant from this table are the job openings which have been in the system for over 3 days (temporary and day-hires are not included in these totals). The ES receives most of its job orders on a strictly voluntary basis from employers; however, those employers who have government contracts are required to list job openings. ES employment service representatives (ESRs) perform job development work in the community, but ESRs experience varying degrees of success in getting local employers to list openings with the job service. Because of the reluctance of employers to list jobs and the varying degrees of success by ESRs, these data do not necessarily reflect the entirety (or even a cross-section) of total job opening activity. They do, however, identify at least some of the industries that are currently hiring and indicate the degree of success that the ES has in filling those openings from its applicant pool. In Travis County, construction and retail trade have large numbers of openings on file with ES, including many in the eating and drinking industry.

Table 3-10
Job Openings Listed with the Employment Service
Austin MSA, Texas
First Quarter 1984

SIC (A)	Industry (B)	Total Openings Received (C)	Openings Over 3 Days* (D)	Fill Rate For All Openings (E)	Fill Rate For Over 3 Days Openings (F)
	Total All Industries	27,453	18,088	62.9	44.1
...	Agriculture, Forestry, Fishing	850	185	93.9	75.1
...	Mining	83	60	59.0	43.3
...	Contract Construction	6,401	2,992	81.2	60.2
17	Special Trade Contractors	2,539	1,212	79.3	57.0
...	Manufacturing	2,268	1,800	63.8	52.1
20	Food and Kindred Products	71	63	62.0	57.1
22	Textile Mill	8	1	87.5	0.0
23	Apparel	16	13	56.3	46.2
24	Lumber and Wood	631	383	111.4	102.3
25	Furniture/Fixtures	90	78	66.7	50.0
26	Paper/Allied Products	16	11	56.3	36.4
27	Printing/Publishing	254	208	61.8	53.4
28	Chemicals	22	12	68.2	41.7
29	Petroleum/Coal	2	2	50.0	50.0
30	Rubber/Plastics	154	132	96.1	95.5
31	Leather/Leather Products	73	72	24.7	23.6
32	Stone, Clay, Glass	125	78	72.0	55.1
33	Primary Metals	9	9	88.9	88.9
34	Fabricated Metals	187	149	68.4	60.4
35	Machinery exc. Electric	154	154	54.5	54.5
36	Electric and Electronic	232	216	55.2	52.3
37	Transportation Equipment	36	35	61.1	60.0
38	Instruments	93	93	31.2	31.2
39	Misc. Manufacturing	95	91	63.2	61.5
...	Transportation and Utilities	1,439	992	50.0	27.6
...	Wholesale Trade	1,228	742	70.0	50.5
...	Retail Trade	4,434	2,767	64.0	42.7
54	Food Stores	279	242	61.3	55.4
58	Eating and Drinking	1,083	1,019	44.4	41.0
...	Finance, Insurance, Real Estate	1,274	1,057	45.2	34.0
...	Services	4,754	3,980	49.5	39.8
73	Business Services	1,328	855	66.9	48.8
80	Health Services	612	601	51.3	50.6
89	Miscellaneous Services	358	302	50.8	41.7
99	Government, Total	3,035	3,022	26.0	25.8

* Openings over 3 days are considered more long term than total openings which include requests for temporary and day labor.

Source: Texas Employment Commission, ESARS Table 12; Covered Wages and Employment, 1st Quarter 1984.

An industry with a low fill rate may give an indication of a skill shortage area. Any single explanation of why a job opening remains unfilled is risky. Openings may remain unfilled for various reasons: (1) the wage rate offered is too low; (2) the experience or education required is too high; or (3) there is a lack of trained workers to fill the position. It is up to the local analyst to research the local labor market and determine why an opening remains unfilled.

Mass Layoff and Plant Closings

The final indicator important to understanding current economic trends is the identification of a major layoff or plant closing. Although some job opening activity may still occur in key skill areas, industries which experience major layoffs or plant closings represent the worst environment for job opening potential. Mass layoffs are generally reported in the local daily newspaper or other business journals. A thorough analyst will make a habit of reviewing the local business pages for just such phenomena. The ES operates a voluntary reporting of significant layoffs (commonly known as the ES-235 report). Because of its voluntary nature, and the fact that the layoff, in most cases, must exceed 100 employees to be significant, this report is not a comprehensive chronicle of layoff activity. As a result of recent Job Training Partnership Act (JTPA) legislation, several states, notably Texas, are operating pilot programs under the sponsorship of BLS to identify mass layoffs through the UI reporting system. Should this program prove successful, detailed reports of major layoffs will be readily available.

Step 5
Prioritizing Key Leading Industries

After reviewing the available data recommended by the industry analytical process, the analyst is in a position to identify and rank those industries which exhibit the greatest job opening potential. This process should be based on information similar to the economic indicators which have already been discussed, i.e., total employment, change in employment, current job openings, hours and earnings, potential new hires, employment projections, business establishments, change in establishments, etc. As the data are carefully studied, generally there will be several industries which seem to rank highly in many of the major indicators.

At this stage it may be helpful to construct a summary table whereby each industry can be examined side-by-side with its various indicators. The industries might be listed in columnar form down the left-hand side of a table, with each indicator that is to be incorporated listed across the top. Pertinent data should then be inserted into the respective cells on the table. Such a summary table allows the analyst to better understand the local industry setting.

As the analyst begins the prioritizing process, it is important to remember that all indicators are not equally significant in identifying job opening potential. Some indicators, such as historical change in employment and current employment, should be weighted more heavily. The analyst should determine in advance how important each indicator is in the process of assessing employment potential. The selection of the top 10 or so industries in the prioritizing process should focus on those which the analyst feels reflect greater job opening potential. To reiterate, this does not mean that industries in the second group of 10 or those further down the industry list do not possess any job opening potential. It is important to remember that this is a *prioritizing process* and does not eliminate other industry sectors.

The authors have automated an Industrial Evaluation Model which is designed to execute on a microcomputer the exact ranking and prioritizing process outlined in this chapter. The model uses nine economic indicators including current employment, change in employment, employment projections, coefficients of specialization, number of business establishments, and several national industry indicators to rank order each 2-digit SIC industry in a local (county or larger) economy. Such a model helps to organize and simplify the task of gathering data and rank ordering industries on the basis of that data. (Appendix 3 presents the model in greater detail.)

Step 6
Identifying Local Employers

While the identification of key leading industries in a local economy is essential to job placement and other activities, the process is uniquely designed to identify specific employers with greater job opening potential. Using the prioritized list of key leading industries developed in steps 1-5, the final step is identifying those specific firms which comprise the key leading industries. Most sources of employer listings categorize firms by SIC code. Therefore, armed with the SIC code of the key leading industries, the analyst may consult a number of sources.

The most comprehensive employer listing is the employer master file from the ES-based Covered Wages and Employment program. This file, maintained by the ES in the research section, has the name, address, employment level and tax account number of each firm that pays Unemployment Insurance taxes. Confidentiality laws prohibit publishing this file; however, some information may still be gleaned from it. In Texas the ES can provide an employer listing by 4-digit SIC code on a county basis which includes an employment size class range. It is up to the practitioner to identify the addresses and contact person(s) within each firm. The telephone book is probably the best source of addresses, and several publications have been developed to help the analyst translate SIC code titles into Yellow Page directory categories. The most useful of these has been published by the California State Occupational Information Coordinating Committee (SOICC).

Where the ES master employer file is not available, employer names may still be accessed through various sources. Most states publish a directory of manufacturers which provides names and addresses of employers in the manufacturing sector. Dun and Bradstreet publishes two volumes, the *Million Dollar Directory* and *Middle Level Directory* of headquartered firms with sales in excess of $1 million and $500,000, respectively. Most chambers of commerce have membership directories which can prove useful to identify local employers. In many states, publications which provide listings of employers are compiled by various sources.

In Travis County, a leading industry is SIC 367. Employers within SIC 367 can be gleaned from either the employer master file or the *1983 Directory of Texas Manufacturers,* published by the University of Texas Bureau of Business Research. The following list of SIC 367 employers is from these two sources:

1) Advanced Micro Devices MOS Div.
2) Cryco Quartz, Inc.
3) Motorola Inc. (Semiconductor Products)
4) Sector Integrated (Circuits Division)
5) Worden Products, Inc. Silicon Division
6) Tracor, Inc.
7) Austin Circuits, Inc.
8) T-F Electronics, Inc.
9) Christian Manufacturing, Inc.
10) White Instruments, Inc.

Although SIC 367 has experienced significant growth over the study period, this does not guarantee that each *firm* within this industry is also expanding. However, the industrial analysis process should provide sufficient information on the local economy and the specific industry to improve the employer contact strategy. Even if each employer may not be hiring, there is much greater likelihood that SIC 367 employers will be hiring than employers selected randomly or those who fall in stable or declining industries.

Linking Industry Analysis
with Occupational Structure

If the purpose of performing an industrial analysis is to achieve a better understanding of the local industrial structure and to identify industries and employers with greater employment potential, Steps 1 through 6 described above should prove useful. Analysis of a local economy can be done at several levels of industrial detail, depending on the availability of data and necessity of greater detail. For most purposes, analysis at the 2-digit SIC level is sufficient and should provide considerable insight into the workings of the local economy.

Analysis at the Three-Digit Level

Although major division or 2-digit analysis can provide a good understanding of the potential strengths and weaknesses of local industries, it is not sufficiently detailed to enable the monitoring of important facets of the industry. For example, within a growing 2-digit (SIC) industry there may be several 3-digit industries which are not performing well. The greater industry detail included in the analysis, the more accurate and complete will be the analysis of the local economy. Moreover, if an occupational analysis (see chapter 4) is to be performed in conjunction with the industry profile, *there are certain data constraints which mandate 3-digit industry detail.* While many states provide OES industry staffing patterns at the 2-digit level, several publish the staffing patterns only for selected 3-digit industries. If this is the case, industry analysis must be carried out to the 3-digit SIC level in order to access industry staffing patterns which may then be crossed over into occupational analysis.

Within a 2-digit local industry there will generally be several key 3-digit industries which comprise the bulk of employment and economic activity. These can be easily measured by calculating the percent of employment represented by each 3-digit industry within the 2-digit category. Other indicators, besides employment, which can be used include (1) historical employment patterns, and (2) the size and number of business establishments.

The information in table 3-11 is provided in tabular form for SIC 36 electric and electronic equipment and SIC 73 business services. Both of these industries were selected by the authors as being in the top 10 industries in Travis County with respect to job opening potential. To gain a greater understanding of the nature of these two sectors and eventually to identify the occupational opportunities within each industry, 3-digit analysis is performed. Ideally, a 3-digit profile should be constructed for each 2-digit industry identified in the top 10 industries in the local community. Unfortunately, the availability of local area data is greatly restricted at the 3-digit level of detail, and the analyst may have to rely on various other data sources and extrapolate existing data to get an accurate profile.

Table 3-11 shows that, within SIC 36, the SIC 367 electronic components industry predominates, with almost 86 percent of total SIC 36 employment in Travis County. Not only does electronic components dominate the 2-digit category, it is responsible for almost 90 percent of the growth in SIC 36 between 1981 and 1984. This is an important example of the value of 3-digit analysis of key leading industries, since the skills required of workers in electronic components SIC 367 may be considerably different from those for electrical-industrial apparatus SIC 362. Milwaukee, Wisconsin, for example, also has high levels of employment in SIC 36. Milwaukee's 3-digit concentration is in SIC 362, which is the production of motors and generators and is closely tied to the automotive industry. Travis County's concentration in SIC 367, the production of semiconductors and related equipment, is closely tied to the production of computers. In monitoring the national and international events which could have an impact on local employment, these two areas are very different.

Table 3-11
Industrial Profile of Employment
for Selected 3-Digit Industries
Travis County, Texas
First Quarter 1981 and 1984

SIC (A)	Industry (B)	Employment 1981 (C)	Employment 1984 (D)	Percent of Employment 1984 (E)	Employment Change 1981-1984 (F)	Reporting Units 1984 (G)
36	Electric and Electronic Equip.	5,154	8,404	100.00%	3,250	48
361	Electric Distributing Equip.	60	78	.93	18	*
362	Electric Industrial Equip.	25	41	.49	16	*
363	Household Appliances	0	*	*	*	*
364	Electric Lighting and Wiring	0	*	*	*	*
365	Radio and TV Receiving Equip.	10	11	.14	1	*
366	Communication Equip.	647	946	11.26	299	11
367	Electronic Components	4,336	7,218	85.89	2,882	24
369	Misc. Electric Equip.	76	99	1.18	23	3
73	Business Services	9,131	13,677	100.00	4,546	851
731	Advertising	301	439	3.21	138	49
732	Credit Reporting	169	187	1.37	18	10
733	Mailing, Reproduction	322	496	3.63	174	60
734	Services to Buildings	1,440	2,203	16.11	763	93
735	News Syndicates	28	28	.21	0	3
736	Personnel Supply Services	1,516	2,457	17.97	941	51
737	Computer and Data Processing	1,021	2,305	16.86	1,284	130
739	Misc. Business Services	4,334	5,562	40.67	1,228	455

* potential disclosure of individual firm's identity prohibits publishing this data.

Source: Texas Employment Commission, Covered Wages and Employment, 1981, 1984.
         Department of Commerce, County Business Patterns, 1982.

Within business services SIC 73, there are several 3-digit industries which have contributed heavily to the growth of the Travis County sector. Employment in computer and data processing services SIC 737 has more than doubled over the most recent 3-year period and led the expansion of this industry. Personnel supply (manpower) services and services to buildings have also shown excellent growth. The largest 3-digit industry in business services is miscellaneous business services SIC 739. Disclosure laws at the 4-digit SIC level prevent the use of ES-202 data for further analysis, but *County Business Patterns* identifies this sector as dominated by research and development laboratories and management and public relations services. The occupational structure, and therefore the demand for labor, is quite different for services to buildings SIC 734 compared to computer and data processing SIC 737.

In most cases, one or more of the 3-digit industries within a 2-digit sector will show some decline in employment over the study period. Such was not the case in the high growth study area, Travis County. If there is a decline in employment in a particular 3-digit sector, this should be duly noted by the analyst as it may affect employment and training or job development efforts within a local area.

A Concluding Note

The quantitative analysis presented here should be augmented with information on the business and economic outlook for selected industries, such as provided in the *U.S. Industrial Outlook Handbook*. It is also useful to monitor business news events reported in local newspapers or national magazines, since they often include information on developments which affect the prosperity of national or local industries. In perusing these periodicals, it should be remembered that individual firms are merely members of an industrial category, and events which affect a single firm may indeed affect the industry as a whole. Such national newspapers as the *Wall Street Journal* also monitor and report on a variety of situations which affect the national economy.

With a priority listing of 2- and 3-digit industries which should have greater potential for job openings, the stage is set for making the transition into occupational analysis. This process begins by identifying the occupational structure of the key leading industries previously identified, and working through systematic steps to identify those occupations which have the greatest potential for job openings. Occupational analysis is discussed in the following chapter.

Selected Chapter Bibliography

Armington, Catherine and Marjorie Odle. "Small Business—How Many Jobs." *The Brookings Review* (Winter 1982).

Bradey, William R. and Albert E. Schwenk. "Wage Rate Variation by Size of Establishment." *Industrial Relations* 191, 2 (Spring 1980).

Bendavid, Avrom. *Regional Economic Analysis for Practitioners.* New York: Praeger, 1974.

Burton, John F. Jr., Lee K. Benham, William M. Vaughn, III, and Robert J. Flanagan. *Readings in Labor Market Analysis.* New York: Holt, Rinehart and Winston, 1971.

Cohen, Malcolm S. *New Hire Rates—A New Measure.* Ann Arbor: Institute of Labor and Industrial Relations, University of Michigan, February 1979.

Dow, Louis A. *Business Fluctuations in a Dynamic Economy.* Columbus: Charles E. Merrill, 1968.

Greene, Richard. "Tracking Job Growth in Private Industry." *Monthly Labor Review* (September 1982).

Hall, R.D. "Turnover in the Labor Force." *Brookings Papers on Economic Activity* 13 (1972).

_____ and David M. Lillien. *The Measurement and Significance of Labor Turnover.* National Commission on Employment and Unemployment Statistics. Washington: Government Printing Office, 1979.

Herzog, Henry W. and Richard J. Olsen. "Shift Share Analysis Revisited: The Allocation Effect and the Stability of Regional Structure." *Journal of Regional Science* 17, 3, (1977).

Hewings, Geoffrey. *Regional Industrial Analysis.* New York: St. Martin's, 1979.

Hirsch, Werner Z. *Urban Economic Analysis.* New York: McGraw-Hill, 1973.

Hoover, Edgar. *An Introduction to Regional Economics.* New York: Alfred Knopf, 1975.

Knight, R.V. *Employment Expansion and Metropolitan Trade.* New York: Praeger, 1973.

Mangum, Garth and David Snedeker. *Manpower Planning for Local Labor Markets.* Salt Lake City: Olympus, 1974.

Martin, Howard, editor. *Chamber of Commerce Research Activities.* Washington: American Chamber of Commerce Researchers Association, 1975.

Pettman, Barrie O. *Labor Turnover and Retention.* New York: Halsted, 1975.

Price, James. *The Study of Turnover.* Ames, IA: The Iowa State University Press, 1977.

Ragan, James F., Jr. "Turnover in the Labor Market: A Study of Quit and Layoff Rates." *Economic Review.* Federal Reserve Bank of Kansas City, May 1981.

Rees, Albert. *The Economics of Work and Pay.* New York: Harper and Row, 1973.

Standard Industrial Classification Manual 1972. Office of Management and Budget. Washington: Government Printing Office, 1972.

Sum, Andrew and Bennett Harrison. "The Theory of 'Dual' or Segmented Labor Markets." *Journal of Economic Issues,* 13, 3, (September 1979).

Texas Employment Commission, Economic Research and Analysis. *Covered Employment and Wages, 1974-1984.*

Texas Employment Commission, Economic Research and Analysis. *Monthly Labor Market Information Newsletter,* (April 1984).

Texas Employment Commission, Economic Research and Analysis, *Area Occupational Demand Forecast—1984,* (1981).

Zell, Steven P. "Interpreting Recent Labor Market Developments." *Monthly Review.* Federal Reserve Bank of Kansas City, March 1975.

Zell, Steven P. "A Labor Market Primer. *Monthly Review.* Federal Reserve Bank of Kansas City, January 1975.

Chapter 4
An Integrated Approach
to Identifying Occupational
Job Opportunities

Introduction

There are many circumstances in which an analysis of occupational job opportunities might be useful. One consideration is that an occupational analysis should identify "growth" occupations. In its most restrictive use, the term "growth" refers specifically to increases in the demand for workers with certain occupational skills. However, it is also generally assumed that there always exist at least some occupational areas for which employers have unmet needs. For these same occupations, the collection of presently available skilled workers often cannot meet the current or near future requirements of local employers. From this broader perspective, a growth occupation is one in which employer demand for skilled individuals in a given occupation is expanding or one where demand exceeds the available supply of trained workers in the local labor market. Consequently, if a number of growth occupations can be identified, they would comprise a group of occupations for which unemployed individuals or new labor force entrants can be trained with a greater probability of obtaining a job after the training period.

75

The task of identifying growth occupations is not a simple one, especially given the nature of existing occupational data. Analyzing the local occupational supply/demand condition requires an understanding of current occupational employment, current unfilled job openings, the existing and potential pool of occupational skills, and the complex relationships between existing wage rates and labor availability/employer needs. Although these information categories are hardly new to employment and training professionals, limitations of existing data sources make it difficult to quantify the results.

Analytical Approaches

There are two basic approaches to identifying growth occupations in a given local area:

(1) an industrial/occupational analytical process, as presented in this monograph; and
(2) a supply/demand analysis resulting in the calculation of equilibrium rates.

Both approaches discussed in this chapter are premised on the fact that the demand for workers in any occupation is a direct function of the demand for the goods or services which those occupational skills combine to produce. The demand for labor is a derived demand; without the demand for goods or services produced by a firm or industry, there would be no need for workers in occupations of any kind. Furthermore, to produce a particular good or service, some combination of occupational skills is generally required. That combination is often unique to the production of a particular good or service. The process introduced in this chapter, therefore, begins with the leading industries identified in a local economy. The occupational skills distribution, or staffing pattern, of each industry is then determined. The intermediate result is a list of occupations with job opportunities; these occupations are integral to the production of the good or service identified to be in demand. It is at this point that, depending on the purpose for determining demand occupations, other qualitative information is incorporated. The available supply of trained workers, as well as prevailing wage rates, occupational projections, working conditions, career ladder, etc., are part of the final qualitative analysis.

The following section presents an overview of supply/demand analysis. While acknowledging that there is much theoretical and some technical merit to the supply/demand ratio approach to identifying growth occupations, the purpose of the remainder of this chapter is to present a full discussion of the industrial/occupational analytical approach.

Supply/Demand Analysis: Approaches and Concerns

Much of the current emphasis in determining demand occupations (with education or employment and training implications) involves establishing a short-run supply/demand equilibrium status for each occupation in a local economy. The major difficulty of supply/demand ratios is in understanding and measuring the various market dynamics, or *flows,* which constantly affect the short-run *stock* of available supply and demand for workers. Calculating these ratios is further complicated by a lack of available data for assessing certain key components of both available supply and available demand, as well as by occupational coding structure mismatches.

There are two temporal considerations in calculating an occupational supply/demand ratio: (1) a *current* measure of the existing equilibrium situation, and (2) a *projection* of both occupational supply and demand conditions.

A current measure represents the *existing stock* of both labor supply and demand. On the supply side, the stock of existing supply includes those persons who are employed in a specific occupation plus those who are unemployed with specific skills and are actively seeking work, at a given point in time at prevailing wages. Both of these components can be estimated using existing data sources (see figure 4-1). The stock of occupational demand is represented by current occupational employment plus current unfilled job openings (again, according to existing wages). Although it is possible to measure current employment using existing data sources, historically it has proven very difficult to measure the number of current unfilled job openings by either occupational or industrial categories.

For several reasons (including the fact that many job openings are never listed through any formal medium), there has never been an accurate count of the stock of current available job openings. Moreover, because occupational supply/demand ratios are generally used for program planning purposes, they are only useful if the two components (supply and demand) are projected for a consistent time period.

This option, producing a projected supply/demand ratio, historically has been the most widely used approach. A projected ratio involves an analysis and measure of *labor market flows*—those dynamics within a given labor market which affect the level of occupational demand and the available labor supply pool. The structure of these flows is illustrated in figure 4-1. Because there are continual movements into and out of the supply of labor for any specific occupation or geographic area, the flows in the diagram are termed *positive* for additions to the supply pool and *negative* for separations. The *net flows* column represents the net effect of these labor market flows which must be measured in order to estimate a future stock of labor supply by occupation.

Figure 4-1
Current and Projected Occupational Supply
(available supply)

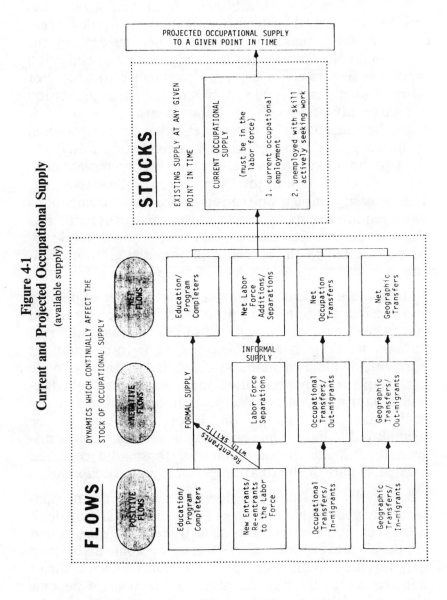

Supply

Current data on education/program completers and enrollees are available through most state education agencies. This source represents a count of persons entering the labor pool with skills acquired through a *formal* education process as they receive a degree, diploma or certificate. For some occupations, formal supply represents a large portion of total supply—especially when state licensure is involved or a specific educational program is essential for occupational competency (e.g., nurse, dental hygienist, or teacher). In many occupations, however, formal supply represents a much smaller portion of total supply, especially where skills may be easily learned on-the-job or for those occupations which require few specific skills. Also, there exists little empirical evidence which estimates the proportion of total supply represented by the formal supply in any given occupation.

Much more difficult to estimate is the number of persons who are new entrants or reentrants to the labor force and have skills gained through informal mechanisms (or, perhaps, no skills at all). These net labor force additions represent an unknown quantity, and their contribution to the total supply for any occupation varies according to the particular nature of the occupation. Although most new entrants and reentrants to the labor force tend to be unemployed initially while engaging in job search, it is difficult to estimate the percentage of those who could be counted as part of the total supply of a given occupation.

By far the most difficult flows to measure are occupational and geographic transfers. This is particularly difficult at the local level where flows tend to be more exaggerated and people move quickly across local geographic boundaries (i.e., traveling to another state or region is more difficult than moving to the next county). The number of persons who are qualified and seeking employment in one occupation while currently employed in another is almost impossible to estimate. For occupations requiring no formal training and few specific skills, the available labor force is often defined by the wage rate offered by a specific employer or the location of a specific job opening. In other words, the parameters of the count of net occupational transfers are in continual flux.

Geographic transfers are equally difficult to measure. They come in two basic forms: (1) transfers into an area with a job already in hand, and (2) transfers into an area seeking employment. In the second case, these individuals could fall either in the new entrants category if they are seeking immediate employment with current skills or into the education/program completer category if they are postponing employment for additional training. In the case of part-time workers concurrently engaging in additional formal training, these persons would be extremely difficult to estimate.

It is notable that there may be a significant overlap of persons across occupational categories in real life situations. This overlap, combined with a dearth of appropriate data, makes estimating occupational supply so difficult. Most current attempts at measuring supply have settled for estimating as many of these flows as possible and eliminating double counting.

Although these measures might not be an accurate reflection of occupational supply, they do have some merit in at least the consistency of their approach toward occupations. Unfortunately, because the level of supply and contributions of any one flow may vary considerably according to the occupational skills required, this feature tends to be overshadowed. Given the existing state of available data, estimating projected occupational supply is one of the most difficult tasks facing a labor market analyst.

Demand

On the demand side, projected estimates of occupational demand have generally been developed according to the two major ways job openings occur: growth and replacement (labor turnover). These estimates are actually surrogates for true "demand," since wages are assumed in the analytical model. By estimating the number of job openings due to expected economic growth and those due to labor turnover, projected occupational employment estimates can be generated. It is important to note that, while the procedure of developing occupational employment projections is relatively straightforward, this does not represent a complete measure of projected occupational demand. Projected demand must account for *current job openings*. Since current job openings are not represented in the base year data for projections (only current employment) there will at any given time be current job openings which are not projected or measurable. The measure of projected occupational employment is, however, often used as a surrogate measure of projected occupational demand (see figure 4-2).

Improvements in data collection, cross-walking techniques, and data manipulation are helping many states to estimate more accurate supply/demand ratios. The preceding concerns, however, have not been resolved successfully; calculating these ratios does not provide an alternative to the analysis of industrial sectors with job opening potential. Furthermore, there is no one list of demand occupations for any geographic area—each group or agency has its own concerns and restrictions regarding specific occupational wage rates, career ladders, training appropriateness, provisions for handicapped persons, etc. Even if the exact supply/demand equilibrium position could be ascertained for an occupational category, by using this approach the analyst still would not be able to identify the industries and firms employing these workers. Because employer files are accessed only through the SIC system (aside from random or alphabetical lists), the industrial categories in which growth occupations are employed must first be identified in order to pinpoint individual employers.

Figure 4-2

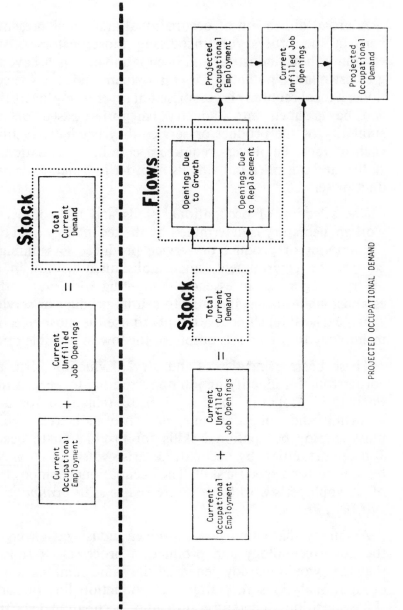

CURRENT STOCK OF OCCUPATIONAL DEMAND

Stock

Current Occupational Employment + Current Unfilled Job Openings = Total Current Demand

Stock

Current Occupational Employment + Current Unfilled Job Openings = Total Current Demand

Flows

Openings Due to Growth

Openings Due to Replacement

Projected Occupational Employment

Current Unfilled Job Openings

Projected Occupational Demand

PROJECTED OCCUPATIONAL DEMAND

Occupational Analysis

A broad dimension of occupational analysis is presented here in the process of uncovering those sectors of the economy, both industrial and occupational, which have the greatest relative potential for employment. With few exceptions, a local economy is comprised of several employers that can be grouped into industry categories based on the similarity of the product or service they produce. In turn, each of these employers requires a certain combination of skilled and unskilled individuals in order to generate its product or service.

The selection of occupational skills and the number of workers necessary is determined by the technology used and the amount of product or service produced. Assuming a competitive environment, an establishment within an industry category is, in essence, competing with every other establishment in that industry to sell its product or service. Thus, each establishment attempts to use the most effective technology to provide its output at the lowest possible price.

These basic principles of industry production form the cornerstone for identifying job opportunities by occupation. Each local economy consists of firms (clustered for data reporting and collection purposes into industries) which · must employ occupational skills for production to occur. Job opportunities, by occupation, arise when an employer has a need for a specific skill. The occupational composition of an employer's workforce is referred to as its *occupational staffing pattern.*

Assuming that employers in a given industry use roughly the same technology and production processes, it follows that they would employ generally the same combination of occupational skills for, at least, production line or semi-skilled positions. Therefore, instead of occupational staffing patterns for each employer, a staffing pattern can be generated which represents the combination of occupational skills that is generally representative of the overall (detailed) industry. In addition, it is usually found that the industry's staffing pattern is representative of both large and medium sized firms. Despite the size of the employer's total workforce (the firm may need more or fewer of each occupational skill depending on how much it is producing), there is still required the same general combination of skills as other employers in the industry.

From this background, it is apparent that if a firm (or all firms in an industry category) is expanding, job opportunities will occur in most occupational skill areas which that firm employs. It follows that, instead of just identifying occupations in which there is a supply/demand imbalance, legitimate efforts could be made to recognize industry sectors which are expanding, identify the occupational staffing patterns of those industries, and thereby determine the occupational job openings most likely to occur in that sector.

The distinction between growth occupations and occupations with greater employment *potential* is significant. The approach presented here places greater emphasis on selecting occupations with greater potential for *numerous,* rather than rapidly growing, occupational opportunities. In this approach, several occupations should emerge which cross over a number of industry lines and have high transferability between industries. Limiting the occupational analysis to growth occupations would disregard the large number of potential job openings that emerge in occupational areas which are not growing rapidly but represent a far greater share of overall employment. Finally, this approach focuses on occupations and job openings in the same manner in which they occur in the labor market. In other words, job openings occur through a combination of growth and replacement needs. For the same reasons, occupational requirements are functions of these same phenomena. (The previous discussion of local industrial analysis highlighted the concept of employee separations and resulting job openings.)

Combining Industrial and
Occupational Analysis: Overview

Earlier reference was made to the integrated approach used here in identifying the industrial and occupational sectors of the local economy which have the greatest potential for job opportunities. Figure 4-3 presents this approach. As the flow chart indicates, each of these subareas is linked to other parts of the system. Theoretically, analysis may begin at any point and proceed, such that the whole system is brought into focus. However, there is an approach which is preferable to selecting a starting point at random.

This overall objective of getting to the "meat" of the industry/occupation analytical process is best accomplished by beginning with *industry analysis.* A thorough industry analysis will result in a hierarchical listing of local area industries based on job opportunity potential.

Once the analyst has worked through the various steps of industry analysis and developed a list of key leading industries, the analytical procedure turns to identifying the occupational structure of those industries. For this purpose, an industry/occupation employment matrix is required. Two such matrices are available: one is based on the Occupational Employment Statistics (OES) statewide survey (the OES-based matrix for participating states) and the other is derived from national staffing patterns developed from a combination of OES and the Census of Population (Census-based matrix). In most cases, the state OES-based matrix should be consulted where it is available, since it represents the staffing patterns unique to the particular state and is recognized as the more statistically accurate and comprehensive employment matrix.

Figure 4-3
Recursive Labor Market Flows

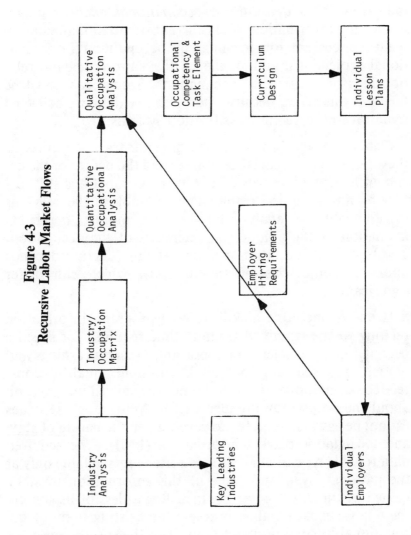

The first step in occupational analysis is to collect and synthesize the available quantitative information as it pertains to the selected occupations which comprise the key leading industries. This *quantitative occupational analysis* hinges upon such information as (1) current occupational employment, (2) current job openings by occupation, (3) occupational projections, and (4) the relative supply/demand relationships of the selected occupations. Special care must be taken at this stage, because the necessary data are collected from several different classification systems.

Qualitative analysis involves more abstract variables as they relate to the local labor market and the nature of the occupation. Having narrowed the list of occupations still further by analyzing the employment outlook in the previous stage, qualitative analysis allows for a more in-depth examination of the unique characteristics of the occupation. The type of information included at this juncture depends upon the objectives of the analysis, which can differ significantly.

If one is operating a skill training program, information relating to the length of training time required for specific occupational proficiency is important. Data on earnings and hours, advancement potential, training qualifications, related occupational fields and other specialized information about the occupation are also useful. Many of these issues cannot be assessed readily, however, given the nature of state and local labor market information (LMI). The required data for this type of analysis most often are available only at the national level, and some of this information must be gained by direct employer contact. Regardless of its source, the analyst must be able to access the existing body of occupational information and tailor it to the specific needs of the program.

The Bureau of Labor Statistics has developed a procedure to estimate the number of job openings arising as workers leave their occupations. Using the national Current Population Survey (CPS) as a data base, occupational separation and replacement rates are computed and projected to 1990 by the Bureau. While these data are important for analyzing *occupational* separations and describing future employment opportunities at the national level, other methods are most appropriate for *industrial* analysis at the local level.

A Final Note on the Integrated Approach

The remaining four stages of the process model represent major linkages with the educational community and are clearly elements of operational planning. Initially, a program must assess *occupational competencies* and determine the skills required of employable program graduates. Ideally, these should be employer-driven where job-specific (e.g., vocational) training is involved. These competencies are then reflected in the development of the *curriculum* and in *individual lesson plans.* Hopefully, the educational skills acquired by the client will be matched to the *hiring requirements* of employers. Although the educational linkages to industry and occupational analysis are clearly within the jurisdiction of the education community, the essence of this approach is the interdependency of the two systems. Such linkages should be clearly understood by practitioners in the fields of labor market analysis and education.

The Occupational Process Model

The analytical process used to study the occupational structure of a local area and identify occupational areas with greater relative employment potential is very similar to that employed in industrial analysis. This adaptive process flows logically from the identification of growth industries to the determination of potential occupational job vacancies within key leading industries. As with the industrial process model, the identification of potential occupational openings is a step-by-step approach. The analysis involves the collection, organization, review and interpretation of available labor market information. This should be combined with qualitative information concerning unique local occupational conditions and hiring requirements. Quantitative labor market information should be augmented with the judgment of experienced labor market analysts and direct employer contact to determine the unique industrial/occupational structure, job availability, and particular occupational characteristics of local jobs.

Occupational Classification Systems

It is essential before the process is begun that the researcher understand the vagaries of occupational classification systems. As indicated earlier, occupational LMI is gathered and presented under a number of different classification systems, including the Occupational Employment Statistics (OES) program, the Census coding systems, the Dictionary of Occupational Titles (DOT) system, the Guide to Occupational Exploration (GOE) codes, and the U.S. Office of Education official coding structure, known as the Classification of Instructional Programs (CIP) system. Additional coding systems under which assorted occupational supply data are collected include the State/National Apprenticeship Program (SNAPS) codes, the Higher Education General Information Statistics (HEGIS) program, and the Vocational Education Data System (VEDS). Although these classification systems have many similarities, each possesses unique qualities. The education coding structures, for example, relate to generic program areas and not to specific occupations. Special attention must be paid to insuring that the analysis compares only consistent occupational categories.

There has been an increasing effort to make these occupational coding systems more compatible. As each system was originally designed, there was no standard adopted for universal use. Historically, government agencies developed their own codes which they felt best served their particular needs. Little consideration was given to matching these coding mechanisms, because each department viewed its information and coding system as an independent, functional data base which was of no use or concern to other government data collection agencies. Such "isolationist" attitudes have given rise to the myriad of nonrelated coding systems that has so confounded integrated occupational analysis.

In 1977 the federal government adopted the Standard Occupational Classification (SOC) system as the standard coding mechanism for all data collected and disseminated on occupations. The revised 1980 SOC provides the core to which all future coding systems will relate. With this concept, the BLS will align more closely the Current Population Survey's occupational categories to the SOC, beginning in 1986.

Identifying comparable occupational categories from one classification system to another, generally known as crosswalking, has been made easier by the publication of the newly revised *Vocational Preparation and Occupations* (VPO) manual. The VPO provides quantitative information regarding required mathematical, language and reading skill levels, the specific vocational preparation training (SVPT) time required, and an overview of physical demands for about 14,600 occupations organized under 600 vocational education-related CIP codes. Most important, the VPO allows for crosswalking between CIP codes, the fourth edition DOT, the 1980 Census codes, the 1980 SOC codes, and OES matrix and survey codes. This volume represents a significant step forward in synthesizing data collected under the several classification systems and will provide for a more complete occupational supply/demand system.

Quantitative Occupational Analysis

The first step of occupational analysis is to narrow the field of all possible occupations in order to focus on those which have the greatest potential for job opportunities. Initially, the occupational composition of the key leading industries selected in the industrial analysis process is examined. The Occupational Employment Statistics (OES) industry/occupation employment matrix provides occupational staffing patterns (shown as a percentage of total employment) for each 3-digit SIC industry surveyed in participating states and selected MSAs. (For areas in which the OES-based matrix is not available, the national BLS Census-based I/O matrix may be substituted.) Although the preferred OES-based matrix is more detailed and accurate, use of the national Census-based matrix is a good example of making the best effort with the data available. Also, if an OES-based matrix is not available in the analyst's state, another option is to use the OES matrix from another state with a comparable industrial structure. Although levels of employment differ considerably between states and areas, the staffing pattern percentages should not be markedly different within the same region.

Examination of staffing patterns reveals the occupational categories which represent the greatest levels of employment. The occupational categories with the greater number of jobs require special attention, since they often represent occupations which will add workers in expansionary periods.

Table 4-1 displays the staffing patterns for both SIC 367 and SIC 737 in Texas. The largest occupations are listed for each industry, along with the estimated local employment (calculated from total industry employment). In the example of SIC 367, electronic components, the largest 13 occupations represent 59.4 percent of total electronic components employment. For SIC 737, computer and data processing, the top 13 occupations employ 84.1 percent of total industry employment. It is important to remember that the occupations listed in table 4-1 are classified by OES codes. In many states, numerical staffing patterns codes must be determined in a separate step by referring to the *OES Dictionary of Oc-*

cupations. The occupational titles, definitions, and the complete structure of the OES classification system are detailed in the *OES Dictionary.* If the national census-based matrix is used, the occupational titles and definitions are provided in the two volume set, *Classified Index of Industries and Occupations* and *Alphabetical Index of Industries and Occupations.* Included in these volumes is a crosswalk of census occupational codes to Standard Occupational Classification (SOC) codes.

Table 4-1
Occupational Staffing Patterns
SIC 367 and SIC 737
Travis County, Texas 1984

OES Code (A)	Occupation by Industry (B)	Estimated Local Employment (C)	Percent of Industry Employment (D)
	SIC 367	7,218	100.00
21005	Electrical and Electronics Engineers	1,094	15.15
55U84	Electrical and Electronics Assemblers	661	9.16
32004	Electrical and Electronics Technicians	577	7.99
55U99	Other Assemblers	351	4.86
61368	Secretaries	320	4.44
59002	Semiconductor Processors/Other Semi Skilled	271	3.75
31002	Computer Programmers, Scientific	196	2.71
32003	Drafters	170	2.36
29000	Professional Managers/Analysts	152	2.11
55R74	Electronic Wirers	141	1.96
55U82	Instrument Makers/Assemblers	128	1.78
21006	Industrial Engineers	129	1.79
62003	Production Clerks	97	1.34
	SIC 737	2,305	100.00
61107	Keypunch Operators	344	14.93
10000	Managers and Officers	270	11.72
71000	Sales Representatives	248	10.74
24001	Business Systems Analysts	220	9.54
31001	Computer Programmers, Business	193	8.33
61105	Computers Operators	153	6.60
61368	Secretary	110	4.75
61900	Other Office Clerical	97	4.18
61333	General Office Clerk	91	3.92
61301	Accounting Clerk	69	2.98
31002	Computer Programmers, Scientific	60	2.60
62900	Other Plant Clerical	47	2.00
61109	Peripheral EDP Operators	43	1.85

Source: Texas Employment Commission, Occupational Employment Statistics (OES) Industry Staffing Patterns, 1983.

For illustration purposes, this analysis of occupations will focus only on the key occupations identified in SIC 367. In practice, the analyst will take several of the key leading industries and select the top 10-15 occupations from each. This will provide a much larger and more diverse list of occupations upon which to perform a quantitative analysis to assess employment potential.

Once the occupational composition of a selected leading industry has been identified, analysis of those occupations deals with such employment potential considerations as: (1) the future growth of the occupation, both locally and nationally; (2) current and future levels of local unfilled job openings; (3) current and expected availability of qualified workers in particular occupations; (4) wages and earnings by occupation; (5) average weekly hours; (6) specific vocational preparation training times; and (7) transferability among industry sectors. More qualitative issues, such as measures of job quality, employer hiring requirements, the occupation's specific tasks and responsibilities, promotional opportunities, and occupational hazards are not adequately covered in the existing body of local labor market information. While information exists at the aggregate level that addresses *national* issues of a qualitative nature, specific local information of this sort usually may be gained only through direct employer contact.

The analyst must have the objectives of the occupational analysis clearly in mind in order to select the pertinent quantitative indicators. A successful selection of key leading occupations with good employment potential depends on the analyst's ability to understand the direction of the study and to synthesize all the available information required to anticipate changes in occupational supply and demand conditions and other local socioeconomic trends which directly affect occupational employment.

Occupational Projections

In response to the initial question concerning the future level of employment in a given occupation, the analyst must depend upon occupational projections. The process of generating occupational projections is generally accomplished by projecting employment by industry to a target year and applying those projected industry figures to an industry/occupation matrix. The matrix provides the distribution of the projected industry employment data by occupational staffing patterns and results in employment projections by occupation.

At both the national and state levels, the OES program is the major vehicle for occupational projections. This program, conducted in three separate cycles, is designed to generate industry employment projections, the industry/occupation matrix, and state and local occupational employment projections. In 1981, the Bureau of Labor Statistics relinquished its advisory role in the state and local projections program and provided the states with a software and analytical package known as DASIE (Data Analysis System for Industry Employment). This package was designed to allow each state office to develop its own industry and occupational employment projections.

Current state industry and occupational projections represent a wide range of combined BLS and ES estimating techniques. Most provide reasonable short term projections, provided that the assumptions upon which the projections rest are not violated. Although statewide projections from ES/Research and Analysis staff tend to receive at least some criticism from users, by and large they represent the best available data for statewide or substate industry and occupational employment projections. As a supplemental source, the BLS publishes a bulletin, *Occupational Projections and Training Data,* from which an analyst may obtain national occupational projections for use in comparison with local projections for selected potential leading occupations.

As in the process of determining potential leading industries, the analyst is encouraged to consult several different occupational data sources—not only to acquire specific information, but also to aid in developing a qualitative sense of selected occupations. Several local ES offices provide occupational information (generated from specific local programs) which can be of tremendous value in the analytical process. Many states have additional state-specific publications which deal with statewide unfilled openings, employment opportunities, salary ranges, and other information. In Texas, the Coordinating Board of Texas Colleges and Universities publishes a biennial report, *Postsecondary Educational Supply and Occupational Demand in Texas,* which is useful for counseling and human resource planning efforts. A planner or analyst might find similar sources to be of supplemental value in the analytical process.

Job Bank Openings

In analyzing the local occupational demand situation, it is also valuable to use the local ES Job Bank to determine which occupations have shown local employment activity. Placing orders with the ES by private employers is optional, for the most part, aside from mandatory listings required of federal contractors. Job Bank figures, consequently, may not be representative of employer occupational demand and may be biased toward unskilled or semiskilled occupations. Regardless of this existing bias, Job Bank tabulations are a primary source used to determine local job availability, and they collectively represent one of many sources used to gain an understanding of the occupational structure of employment. Openings received and filled from local employers are reported in the ESARS system. Tables 7A/B, and especially

96A/B (Applicants and Openings by Occupation) are very useful in assessing occupational job openings which are filed by local employers. Table 96B is also useful in determining the number of ES applicants in a local area who are unemployed and possess specific occupational skills. These data are classified by 9-digit DOT codes.

Occupational Supply

The process of estimating local occupational supply is a complex issue. As discussed previously, supply data are collected and organized under several coding systems which make integration difficult. Moreover, many determinants of occupational supply have never been accurately estimated. For example, the number of occupational transfers crossing both geographic boundaries and occupational categories is almost impossible to estimate for the local labor market area. The fewer skills required of the occupation, the more difficult it becomes to measure the number of transfers. Although extensive data are collected for public academic and vocational institutions, little are available on vocational proprietary institutions and employer-specific on-the-job (OJT) training. All of these factors combine to make estimating occupational supply a difficult task. Thus, any attempt to estimate local occupational supply should take these limitations into consideration.

Wages and Earnings

The availability of local wage and earnings data varies considerably from state to state. The Research and Statistics unit of each ES should be consulted to determine the extent to which state and local occupational wage data are collected. Another valuable resource organization is the State Occupation Information Coordinating Committee (SOICC), whose mission is to research and synthesize the myriad of occupational data into a comprehensive system.

There are several additional potential sources of wage and earnings data. Many state economic development agencies maintain area profiles including wage rates for key occupations. Each state also has an agency which is responsible for setting state government employee wage rates. The state classification agency is responsible for researching wage rates for occupations within the state to make state employment compensation comparable to the private sector. Area chambers of commerce often undertake local wage surveys to assist in local economic development efforts. At the federal level, the Bureau of Labor Statistics (BLS) is responsible for several data programs which generate occupational wage data. The BLS Area Wage Surveys and Industry Wage Surveys represent two programs which collect and publish wage and benefits data for selected industries and geographic areas.

The BLS also is responsible for the Current Population Survey (CPS) conducted by the Bureau of the Census. Every year during the month of March an expanded survey is conducted. From the expanded CPS, the BLS recently published a bulletin, *Analyzing 1983 Earnings Data from the Current Population Survey*. This volume includes statewide annual earnings and incomes of workers by occupation. The BLS also provides earnings data that are included for the 200 occupations which comprise the *Occupational Outlook Handbook*.

If state and local occupational wage data are not available, national data should be consulted to identify the *relative* occupational wage. However, it must be recognized that the average may be skewed and that average earnings vary, often significantly, among geographic areas and even for the same occupation in different industries. The degree of unionization, the local industrial structure, and the relative cost of living are but three reasons why wage rates may vary from location to location.

LMI Summary Chart

At this point in the process, it is valuable to assemble a labor market information summary chart for the key occupations comprising the selected potential leading industry. This chart should include a listing of the major occupational categories which staff the key leading industry and appropriate characteristics of each occupation. Indicators to be displayed in tabular form might include current and projected employment, each occupation's percent of total industry employment, average wages, available openings, and the specific occupation classification codes. From this chart, the analyst can more easily synthesize the LMI necessary for targeting occupations with the greatest job potential. Table 4-2, *LMI Occupational Summary Chart for SIC 36, Travis County* displays several key indicators for 13 occupations in SIC 367.

The appropriate criteria for selecting target occupations are determined in the final part of this exercise. For example, if the analyst is planning a public training program, the occupations ultimately selected must provide employment opportunities for both males and females, pay wages at or above minimum program standards, and require a training period which is allowable under program standards. Since the identification of target occupations depends upon several factors, primarily the particular nature of the program's objective, no specific evaluation model will serve all purposes.

For the occupations within SIC 367, there are several key distinctions. The engineering and computer programming occupations generally require a college education or the equivalent of four years of training. This eliminates these occupations as training options, for example, under the Job Training Partnership Act (JTPA). Several occupations are industry specific (e.g., semiconductor processor). This reduces the possibility that, should employment opportunities dry up in SIC 367, skills learned would be

Table 4-2
LMI Occupational Summary Chart for SIC 367
Travis County, Texas 1984

OES Code (A)	Occupations <1> (B)	DOT Code (C)	Est.<1> Travis Cty. Emp. 1984 (D)	% of Industry Emp. (E)	Austin MSA Proj. Net Increase 1978-85 (F)	Job<2> Openings Rec'd (G)	Curr.<2> No. of Unemp. (H)	% Female Emp. <3> (I)	Entry-level Wages/ Earn.<4> (J)	SVP <5> Training Time (K)
21005	Electrical/Electronic Engineer	003.061-010	1,094	15.15	1,000	60	14	5.6%	$26,140 annual	8
55E22	Electrical/Electronic Assembler	726.384-010	661	9.16	650	146	133	48.4	6.75/hour	2
32004	Electrical/Electronic Technician	003.161-014	577	7.99	1,100	8	27	13.0	16,536 annual	7
55199	Other Assembler	714.684-010	351	4.86	1,350	*	*	48.4	6.15/hour	3
61368	Secretary	201.362-030	320	4.44	2,650	1,113	232	99.1	12.096 annual	6
59002	Semiconductor Processor/Other Semi-Skilled	590.684-022	271	3.75	*			48.4	varies	3
31002	Computer Programmer, Scientific	020.167-022	196	2.71	1,550	180	106	29.7	21,480 annual	8
32003	Drafter	003.281-014	170	2.36	450	75	24	19.9	18,840 annual	7
29000	Professional Manager/Analyst	020.067-018	152	2.11	*	7	19	19.2	17,500 annual	7
55R74	Electronic Wirer	729.281-042	141	1.96	*	*	*	48.4	15,000 annual	6
55082	Instrument Maker/Assembler	809.681-010	128	1.78	550	*	*	24.5	14,500 annual	4
21006	Industrial Engineer	012.167-030	129	1.79	100	88	46	8.5	24,276 annual	7
25401	Accountant/Auditor	160.167-010	109	1.51	750	111	104	40.5	19,500 annual	8
62003	Production Clerk	221.382-018	97	1.34	300	*	*	76.1	14,880 annual	4

* data not available

Code	SVP Training Time
1	short demonstration only
2	anything beyond short demonstration up to and including 30 days
3	over 30 days up to and including 3 months
4	over 3 months up to and including 6 months
5	over 6 months up to and including 1 year
6	over 1 year up to and including 2 years
7	over 2 years up to and including 4 years
8	over 4 years up to and including 10 years
9	over 10 years

Source: Texas Employment Commission, Occupational Employment
Statistics Program <1>; ESARS Table 96B <2>.
1980 Census <3>.
Austin Chamber of Commerce <4>.
U.S. Department of Labor, Dictionary of Occupational
Titles, 1974 <5>.

transferable to other industry sectors. Except for engineering, most SIC 367 occupations have a fairly even sex distribution. Most human resource programs, despite the inroads made in nontraditional job training, want to offer training in occupations suitable to both sexes. A balanced mix, in other words, is preferable.

Qualitative Occupational Analysis

Several LMI sources provide supplementary nonquantitative information on occupations. Since these sources deal with occupations at the aggregate (national) level, the information should be tempered with any local area-specific data that have been gathered through direct employer contact, local employer surveys, or other sources. The fourth edition of the *Dictionary of Occupational Titles* (DOT) provides information on the tasks, responsibilities, and fields of specialization that apply to 20,000 occupations. It is an especially valuable resource in designing a specific training curriculum, as well as in more general occupational analysis.

Another volume, which details (1) the physical demands of the occupation, (2) the environmental conditions of the usual workplace, and (3) the relative mathematical and language skills appropriate for the occupation, is the *Selected Characteristics of Occupations Defined in the DOT.* This supplement to the fourth edition of the DOT also provides, for each occupation, the specific vocational preparation training time (SVPT) (i.e., the length of time necessary for preparing an individual, through both classroom and on-the-job training, to be capable of working in the occupation). In the case of employment and training programs, an occupation with a long SVPT may not be acceptable under the program's regulations. This volume is also helpful in counseling persons with specific handicaps or physical disabilities.

In addition to these DOT reference books, the *Occupational Outlook Handbook* provides extensive information on many occupations, including working conditions, employment potential, training and other qualifications, earnings, and related occupations. This reference is familiar to many counselors since it provides detailed information for a wide variety of occupations.

One final reference book which may be of particular importance to employers is the *EEOC Report of Minorities and Women in Private Industry*. This two-volume set is the compilation of employer EEO-1 reports (filed with the Equal Employment Opportunity Commission) on employment by occupation, race, and sex. Employment data are provided at the 2- and 3-digit SIC levels for the nation and at major industry categories for states and MSAs. Each industry category is disaggregated by major occupational group; from there, employment is distributed by sex and race. Thus, this reference provides the occupational structure of each industry, including the occupational distribution of women and minorities, which is particularly valuable to employers who wish to compare the race/sex distribution of their workforce relative to similar firms in their particular geographic area or other areas throughout the country. Program planners can also use this information to identify industries, occupational groups, or geographic areas which hold the greatest employment potential for female and minority clients. Similar EEO data have been collected from the 1980 Census of Population and can be compiled at the county level for each of the 504 census occupations. The National Technical Information Service (NTIS) can provide access to these and other census-based data.

Conclusion

A great deal of labor market information exists which can be analyzed to identify the local occupational structure. Because LMI cannot provide all the local information necessary to make final judgments in analyzing occupational demand, there is often no substitute for a locally experienced analyst to analyze occupations and identify those with greater employment potential. LMI does provide much of the statistical evidence and background documentation necessary for the analyst to stay abreast with changes in occupational fields. Used in conjunction with an organized analytical process, it also allows time and expense to be minimized in the selection of potential occupational employment opportunities worthy of special program emphasis, career counseling, or recruiting efforts.

Selected Chapter Bibliography

Alphabetical Index of Industries and Occupations. U.S. Bureau of the Census, Superintendent of Documents. Washington, 1980.

Analyzing 1981 Earnings Data from the Current Population Survey, Bureau of Labor Statistics. Washington.

Armington, Catherine and Marjorie Odle. "Small Business—How Many Jobs." *The Brookings Review* (Winter 1982).

Armknecht, Paul A. "Job Vacancies in Manufacturing 1969-73." *Monthly Labor Review* (August 1984).

Classification of Instructional Program (CPI). National Center for Education Statistics, U.S. Office of Education, Washington, 1982.

Classified Index of Industries and Occupations. U.S. Bureau of the Census, Superintendent of Documents, Washington, 1980.

Career and Labor Market Information: Key to Improved Individual Decision Making. Columbus: The National Center for Research in Vocational Education, Ohio State University, March 1980.

Cohen, Malcolm S. *New Hire Rates—A New Measure.* Ann Arbor: Institute of Labor and Industrial Relations, University of Michigan, February 1979.

Counting the Labor Force. National Commission on Employment and Unemployment Statistics, September 1979.

Data Analysis System for Industry Employment (DASIE). Bureau of Labor Statistics, U.S. Department of Labor, Washington, 1981.

Dictionary of Occupational Titles (DOT). Fourth Edition. Employment and Training Administration, U.S. Department of Labor, Washington, 1977.

Elttar, M.D and John Saunders. "Measuring Components of Occupational Change." *Growth and Change* (October 1974).

Greene, Richard. "Tracking Job Growth in Private Industry." *Monthly Labor Review* (September 1982).

Guide to Occupational Exploration (GOE). Employment and Training Administration, U.S. Department of Labor, 1979.

Labor Market Information: A Handbook. Salt Lake City: Olympus, July 1979.

Local Area Personal Income. U.S. Department of Commerce, Bureau of Economic Analysis, Regional Economic Measurement Division, July 1980.

National Industry-Occupation Employment Matrix. Bureau of Labor Statistics, U.S. Department of Labor, Bulletin 2086, Vol. I and Vol. II, April 1981.

1981 EEOC Report of Minorities and Women in Private Industry. Equal Employment Opportunity Commission, Washington, 1982.

Occupational Employment Projections for Labor Market Areas: An Analysis of Alternative Approaches. Employment and Training Administration. U.S. Department of Labor, R&D Monograph 80, 1981.

Occupational Information System (OIS) Handbook. Vol. I. National Occupational Information Coordinating Committee. Washington, 1981.

Occupational Opportunities Information. Wisconsin Department of Industry, Labor and Human Relations, 1979.

Occupational Outlook Handbook. Bureau of Labor Statistics, U.S. Department of Labor, Bulletin 2200, 1984-85.

Occupational Projections and Training Data. Bureau of Labor Statistics, U.S. Department of Labor, 1984-85.

Postsecondary Educational Supply and Occupational Demand in Texas. Coordinating Board, Texas College and University System, Spring 1983.

Ragan, James F. "Turnover in the Labor Market: A Study of Quit and Layoff Rates." *Economic Review,* Federal Reserve Bank of Kansas City, May 1981.

Selected Characteristics of Occupations Defined in the DOT. Employment and Training Administration, U.S. Department of Labor, 1981.

Sommers, Dixie and Carin Cohen. "New Occupational Rates of Labor Force Separation." *Monthly Labor Review* (March 1980).

Standard Occupational Classification (SOC) Manual. Office of Federal Statistical Policy and Standards, U.S. Department of Commerce, Washington 1980.

Stevens, David W. *Unemployment Insurance Beneficiary Job Search Behavior.* Human Resources Research Program, University of Missouri-Columbia, 1979.

Terrie, Walter E. *Occupational Statistics and Socioeconomic Analysis.* Houston: American Statistical Association, August 1980.

The Public Employment Service and Help Wanted Ads. Employment and Training Administration, U.S. Department of Labor, R&D Monograph 59, 1978.

Vocational Preparation and Occupations (VPO). National Occupational Information Coordinating Committee. Washington, 1983.

Wisconsin Occupational Employment Statistics Employment Projections to 1985. Wisconsin Department of Industry, Labor and Human Relations. Madison, WI: 1977.

Chapter 5
Application of LMI
to Career Counseling

Introduction

Of the many ways in which occupational analysis may be applied, none is more important than the use of occupational information in counseling. The labor market operates in a dynamic, constantly evolving environment; only through labor market and occupational information can a career counselor expect to stay abreast of changing occupational opportunities and the functional metamorphosis of existing occupations. It is essential that counselors be aware of where future job opportunities will exist so that they may direct students into occupational fields in which there will be job opportunities when the student finishes the prescribed course of study.

Labor Market Information

Actually, the identification of occupational job opportunities requires the study of many facets of the labor market. This analysis must identify those industries which comprise the local economy and the occupational skills employed, as well as the hiring requirements and other characteristics of the jobs—training and qualifications, wages, hours, working conditions, and advancement potential. Since the guidance counselor is often requested to assist students who may be pursuing jobs in several locations across the country, the key to counseling with labor market information is to understand the best *processes* which can be used in local labor market analysis and the *sources* of information for researching other labor markets.

A guidance counselor receives endless routine questions concerning job opportunities and occupational fields. It is the unconventional question, however, which most often takes the greatest effort to answer. With the myriad of other job duties that a counselor must perform, it is very difficult to devote extensive amounts of time to reading and analyzing labor market information. Consequently, it is important that a counselor master a few simple analytical techniques and understand several key data sources so that those "nonroutine" questions may be answered accurately but without an undue expenditure of time.

Assisting Students

Figure 5-1, which graphically depicts the Student Placement Model, identifies the flow of skill training and job placement activities that must combine to achieve the desired outcome: a student with employable skills finding a job in his/her skill area. Unfortunately, the selection of a skill training curriculum is sometimes made without reference to the existing job market. In those situations where the convenience of *ad hoc* training selection is the norm, the student-job matching process is essentially random. Only under circumstances when the labor market is tight and plentiful jobs exist in most occupational areas does this process appear to work. (In this case, employers are willing to hire even those graduates with marginal skills to meet their manpower needs, but society's resources may be allocated inefficiently.)

However, when the labor market is loose (jobs are less abundant) skill training in the most appropriate occupational field is much more important in placing graduates. As the competition among skilled workers for fewer job openings becomes more intense, the nature and quality of the training curriculum is paramount.

Figure 5-1
Student Placement Model

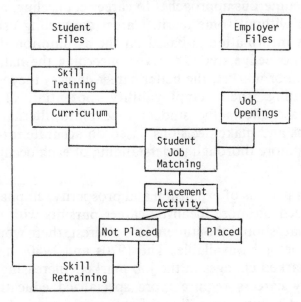

Adapted from K. Kurt Eschenmann and Betty Heath, "Placing the Voc Ed Student." Occupational Outlook Quarterly, Bureau of Labor Statistics, U.S. Department of Labor, 1982.

For efficient use of limited resources, it is essential that those involved in curriculum design and counseling be able to identify local occupational opportunities and hiring requirements in order to increase the percentage of students whose graduation is marked by job placement. In the absence of such analysis, there is an increased likelihood that student graduates may remain unemployed or underemployed with obsolete or inadequate skills to meet employers' current hiring requirements.

Counseling with Labor Market Information

There are numerous approaches to career counseling, and most are not without some merit. Career counseling using labor market information is based on the assumption that the greater knowledge students have concerning the nature of the local labor market, the better career choices they will make regarding their employability potential. This knowledge base allows the student to explore alternative career options and make decisions based on accurate information and a more thorough understanding of each occupational opportunity.

In previous periods of expansion and prosperity, emphasis could be placed on more idealistic career pursuits with the knowledge that, should the student lose interest, there would always be other jobs available. The 1970s and 1980s have ushered in marked changes in the job market. Increasingly, contemporary careers require more specialized education and training. Certain occupational fields, such as mid-level management, which have traditionally offered stable employment are no longer so secure. In addition, several of the fastest growing occupational fields have just recently emerged due to technological advances. Because the number of unemployed persons in 1983 rose to levels comparable with those in the depths of the Great Depression, the competition for available job openings in many skilled and all unskilled occupational areas has been extremely fierce.

Career Counseling

Increasingly, the emphasis of career counseling is to provide students with sufficient information to select career alternatives that meet their preestablished interests and aptitudes as well as develop their employability potential. For this task, both the counselor and the student must understand at least the prominent features of the labor market. If students are considering alternative geographic locations, each area's unique industrial structure and economic base should be considered. Similarly, each industry employs a unique occupational distribution of skills. Thus, if a student wants a job in a certain occupational skill area, he/she must be able to identify those industries and establishments employing that occupation in the local area under consideration. The unique and inextricable interrelationships between geographic areas, industries, employers, occupations, and personal interests and aptitudes are of paramount importance in structuring a student's occupational training plans.

To support the planning and counseling process, two versions of a decisionmaking exercise are explained here which allow the counselor and student to access the most appropriate labor market and occupational information. The first version revolves around a "Circle of Decisions" concept which allows the counselor to explore occupational options from several different perspectives. The large body of available labor market information may be accessed from any of these perspectives. The second version of the counseling exercise uses the same Circle of Decisions concept but provides the counselor with a specific "Decisionmaking Process Matrix." This matrix allows the counselor quickly and systematically to access the LMI pertinent to each approach of the Circle of Decisions.

The Circle of Decisions

In order to use the many career and labor market information sources and reference materials, one of four key decisions must first be chosen: (1) occupational area, (2) industry sector, (3) geographic area, and (4) personal interests and aptitudes. While each decision constitutes a separate approach, any one selection made initially gains access to the available information. Figure 5-2 depicts the basic structure of the "Circle of Decisions."

**Figure 5-2
Circle of Decisions**

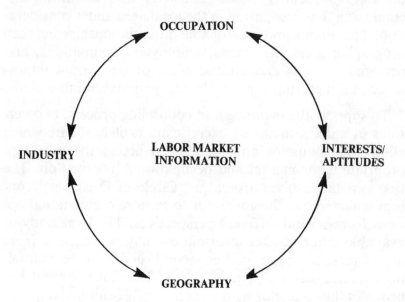

The initial decisions open up a "port of entry" into the decisionmaking process. Upon making the initial decision in any one of these categories, the student gains access to all the information inside the circle. At this point the student can explore further options that are available. For example, if a student is uncertain about his interests, aptitudes, occupational choice, and has no industry preference, but knows for sure that he wants to live in a particular geographic area, the industrial and occupational structure of that area may be ascertained using local LMI.

In another case, if the only certainty is that an individual wants to work in a particular industry (the "television business," for example), this decision will allow access into the circle of information from which the occupational distribution of the television business may be determined. Likewise the geographic areas which have the greatest concentration of employment in the television industry can be determined, and the student may sign up for testing to ascertain if he has an aptitude for any of the occupational areas employed in the television business. The key lies in getting the student to make at least one decision in regard to his career future. As the student and counselor explore the range of opportunities, a key decision may be changed or another made in a different decision area. Each of these four decision areas is explained in greater detail in the following discussion.

Decision Area One: Occupational Area

The choice of a career or occupation to enter is one of the most significant decisions in a person's life. Labor market and occupational information helps the student explore the variety of occupational opportunities which comprise the world of work. Additionally, it provides in-depth information concerning the nature of the occupation's training and qualifications, relative working hours and earnings, and related occupational fields. This information allows the student to explore other areas of interest and discover new occupational fields.

The most comprehensive source of occupational information is the Dictionary of Occupational Titles (DOT). The DOT provides information concerning the nature and tasks of almost every practiced occupation; over 20,000 are classified. There are several reasons to begin occupational exploration with the DOT. Along with its description, a unique DOT coding number is provided for each occupation. This DOT code is the most frequently used occupational coding mechanism; many other information sources are indexed or cross-classified by DOT codes. Beginning with the DOT, the counselor can branch out to several different sources of information which are not as easily accessed from other sources.

Since 1982, federal government occupational publications have been organized and cross-referenced by Standard Occupational Classification (SOC) codes. Unfortunately, there is no *direct* linkage between DOT and SOC codes. However, there are two options for making a cross-reference. The recently published volumes of the *Vocational Preparation and Occupations* (VPO) provide a comprehensive crosswalk between five major coding systems. The hardcopy volumes, however, are organized under Classification of Instructional Program (CIP) code, which is a product of the U.S. Office of Education. This makes the cross-coding process among the other coding systems more difficult. The easiest way to make the DOT to SOC connection is by using the *Occupational Outlook Handbook* (OOH). The OOH provides detailed information for about 250 occupations and was recently organized according to SOC codes. The corresponding DOT codes are also provided in the OOH, and a valuable index is included which allows access to the volume either by SOC or DOT codes. Figure 5-3 clearly depicts these relationships.

The direction of the arrows indicates the direction in which a cross-reference may be made. For example, the one-way arrow between the SOC coding mechanism and the DOT means that, for each SOC code number, the SOC manual provides the corresponding DOT code. However, if one begins with only a DOT code number, appropriate SOC codes are not provided unless they are accessed using the index of the OOH. Although this may appear complex, the actual process of using these three volumes in series is quite simple and can be accomplished with minimal effort and time. Aside from its value as a classification system, the SOC groups its occupations on the basis of the type of work performed. Therefore, it provides a valuable reference for identifying *related occupations*. If a student is interested in a particular occupation but finds the industry or work setting for that occupation is undesireable, he may identify occupations which are similar in nature but may cross into other industry settings.

Figure 5-3

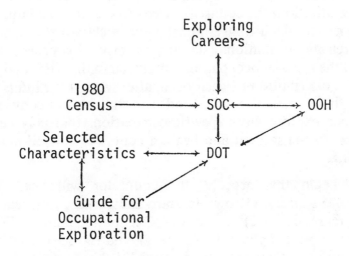

In addition to these three sources, there are several other volumes cited in figure 5-3. The *Exploring Careers* volume, for example, is written as a world-of-work orientation reference, with approximately a junior high school reading level. Although designed for younger students, the publication allows the student to understand the job or occupation as it is experienced by workers. Included are fourteen chapters that correspond to those in the *Occupational Outlook Handbook*.

Decision Area Two: Industry Sector

Counselors often find that many students have not seriously considered any specific occupational area at the time of graduation. Moreover, despite the importance of education and acquiring marketable skills, students often end up seeking relatively low skilled jobs with no advancement potential. However, some students are interested in certain industrial sectors of the local or national economy. For instance, a student may want to consider working in a particular local firm although he is uninformed about job responsibilities and requirements. To assist the student in such a situation, the counselor needs to identify the industry category in which that establishment is classified and then research its occupational staffing pattern. This process will reveal the types of occupations employed in that firm and the present distribution of each occupation within the industry. With these occupations in mind, the student and counselor can then explore those specific occupations that may be of interest to the student and begin a course of education and training.

To begin this process, the counselor will need two reference sources: (1) the Standard Industrial Classification (SIC) manual and (2) an Industry/Occupation matrix. (For a more complete explanation of the I/O matrix, see the section "Quantitative Occupational Analysis" in chapter 4.) The industry designation of a particular local firm may be identified in several ways. The personnel director of the firm probably knows the SIC code under which the firm is classified because of federal and state tax and other data collecting requirements. In a more indirect manner, the industry designation may be determined by identifying the major product or service provided by that firm and referring to the SIC manual. Having identified the major product or service, the SIC manual provides an alphabetical index for both manufacturing and nonmanufacturing industries. In the event that a particular SIC title is unclear, the text of the SIC manual provides a short description of the product or service that is produced.

Armed with a specific SIC industry code and title, the counselor then locates that particular industry title and code on the I/O matrix. If a national census-based employment matrix is consulted, only the specific industry title is used. Where a statewide OES-based matrix is employed, the counselor can use either the SIC code or industry title to access the staffing patterns. Once the staffing pattern has been located, the counselor and student may investigate any or all of the occupational areas that are employed.

Decision Area Three: Geographic Area

For students who are undecided or unenthusiastic about any particular occupational or industrial sector, there are two decision areas which can be accessed. The first of these is the decision concerning geography. That is, where would the student prefer to live? The decision of where one lives has considerable bearing on the occupational or career options available. Most occupational opportunities are unique to the industrial structure of the geographic area in which one resides. Although there are self-employment career options and small business or personal services which can be pursued in almost any area, job opportunities are a function of the local industrial structure. To make a decision regarding where one will live automatically limits the occupational choices to be made and defines where job opportunities will most likely occur. Thus, since the industrial structure of the labor market area defines the available job opportunities (both industrially and occupationally) a student who is undecided in other areas but has made a decision on where to live has automatically taken the first step in making an occupational choice.

There are several sources which detail the current industrial structure and the employment size of the local economy. *County Business Patterns* is a comprehensive source of industry employment data, on a county basis, which also identifies the number of business establishments in each industry and the distribution of business establishments by employee size class. On a less detailed but more current level, the State Employment Security Agency (ES) publishes industry employment data by county. These ES-202 data are available through the local ES office.

Once the industrial structure of a particular geographic area has been determined, there are several choices open to the counselor and the student. They may perform an industry or occupational analysis (as outlined in previous chapters) to identify those areas which appear to have the greatest potential for job opportunities. The student may review the list of local industries and make another decision based on a preference for a particular industry. In this case, the process outlined in Decision Area Two will be useful. Finally, the student may wish to examine the industrial structure of several other geographic areas, either regionally or nationwide.

It is important to remember that, although there may be some employment opportunities in many occupations regardless of the geographic location, the *number* of potential job openings in any occupation will depend on the local industrial structure. For example, in two metropolitan areas of roughly the same population, Pittsburgh and Dallas-Ft. Worth, the former forecast the employment of 195,303 clerical workers in 1985 while Dallas-Ft. Worth anticipated 362,100 clerical employment. The sizable difference can be accounted for by the industrial structure of the Dallas-Ft. Worth metropolitan area, which functions as a regional service center and financial/insurance hub and therefore requires greater levels of clerical support.

Decision Area Four: Interests and Aptitudes

This, the most common approach taken by counselors, helps an indecisive student achieve a better understanding of his own abilities and interests as they relate to occupations. The first three decision areas allow the student to explore many career options based exclusively on what he thinks he may *want* to do for a livelihood. They all involve making decisions from personal interests. The fourth decision area allows the student to explore career options based on various testing mechanisms which identify the student's unexpressed interests and aptitudes. From these aptitude tests, the counselor can identify particular occupational areas for which the student has some natural inclination.

Although there are numerous interests and aptitude testing batteries available, most of them are not directly comparable to any occupational classification used in the LMI system and, therefore, do not directly relate to other resource materials employed in the study of occupational opportunities. There is one key resource volume, however, which has bridged the gap between aptitude testing and occupational analysis. This volume, developed by the U.S. Employment Service, is the *Guide for Occupational Exploration* (GOE). The GOE provides an organizational structure for classifying occupations based on interest areas. Each interest area includes specific DOT occupational codes and titles which are most directly applicable. Several testing batteries have been devised to work within the GOE framework. The General Aptitude Test Battery (GATB) and the Interest Inventory and Revised Interest Check List form a coordinated assessment/occupational exploration system developed by the ES for use in the counseling process. To facilitate use of GATB results with the GOE, a new set of Occupational Aptitude Patterns (OAP) has been developed based on work groups in the GOE. The GOE provides the linkages necessary for the student to explore the various interest areas which comprise the world of work as well as identify particular interest and occupational areas for which the student has demonstrated interest or aptitude through the testing mechanisms. Because there is a direct link with DOT occupational titles, further information and analysis may be performed on any occupational area that is singled out.

It should be emphasized that the process outlined in Decision Area Four does not slight any of the existing aptitude testing batteries. In fact, the Strong-Campbell Aptitude Batteries also work well in conjunction with the GOE. However, some attempt must be made to link the occupational categories used in any aptitude test battery with those classifications employed by the various agencies responsible for occupational data collection and analysis.

The Decisionmaking Process Matrix

As previously noted, LMI can be extremely valuable in the career exploration process. One major difficulty in using LMI is determining *which data sources* one should use in order to derive the desired information. The second major difficulty in using LMI in the counseling process is determining the *sequence* in which the information should be used to assess both occupational characteristics and employment opportunity. The introduction of the LMI Decisionmaking Process Matrix makes both of these problems less troublesome (see figure 5-4). This process matrix both provides a key to accessing the proper LMI resource volume for the desired information and introduces a sequence for using these resources based on the analytical process introduced in chapters 3 and 4.

The use of this matrix is twofold. The counselor can simply determine what type of information is desired, based on the column headings of the matrix, and move to any of the rows to discover the resource volumes which contain that information. The resources have been letter coded, with each

Figure 5-4
LMI Decisionmaking Process Matrix

TYPE OF INFORMATION DESIRED

COUNSELING DECISION AREAS	OCCUPATIONAL TITLE	OCCUPATIONAL DESCRIPTION AND CODE	OCCUPATIONAL PREPARATION AND TRAINING	RELATED OCCUPATIONS	INDUSTRIAL COMPOSITION	OCCUPATIONAL COMPOSITION/STRUCTURE (STAFFING PATTERN)	ANALYZE LOCAL INDUSTRIAL BASE	JOB OPENINGS BY OCCUPATION	PROJECTED OCCUPATIONAL EMPLOYMENT/ OPPORTUNITY	CLIENT APTITUDE/ INTEREST AREAS	WAGE RATES	ADVANCEMENT OPPORTUNITY	INDUSTRIAL TITLE, DESCRIPTION AND CODE
OCCUPATION	1 B,D E,F	2 B,C,D H,J,E	8 C,H,G K	9 D,H,G E	3 A,Q,R		5 N,T,U L	6 K,O H	7 H,L,K S	12 G,J	10 H,M,O	11 H,J,K	4 A,F
INDUSTRY	5 B,D E,F	6 B,C,D H,J,E	9 C,H,G K	10 D,H,G K		4 A,P,R	3 N,T,U L	7 K,O H	8 H,L,K S	13 G,J	11 H,M,O	12 H,J,K	1/2 A,F
INTERESTS/ ATTITUDES	2 B,D E,F	3 B,C,D H,J,E	9 C,H,G K	10 D,H,G E	4 A,Q,R		6 N,T,U L	7 K,O,H	8 H,L,K S	1 G,J	11 H,M,O	12 H,J,I	5 A,F

KEY:
STEPS = NUMBERS
DATA SOURCES = LETTERS

EXAMPLE: 1   STEP ONE
          A,D   SEE RESOURCES A AND D ON LMI DATA BANK

letter representing a resource listing on the LMI data bank (see figure 5-5). For example, once a counselor and student select an occupation about which they desire a more detailed description, they may turn to the process matrix where the counselor will find the volume labeled "occupational description and code." Under this column heading are found the letters "B," "C," "D," "H," "J," and "E." This means that occupational descriptions and their numerical code can be found in the *DOT, Selected Characteristics of the DOT,* the *SOC,* the *VPO,* the *Occupational Outlook Handbook,* and the *Exploring Careers* volume.

The second application of the process matrix is based on use of the counseling decision areas described in the Circle of Decisions. In exploring career options, the student may express curiosity about a particular occupation, industry, or interest area. The process matrix will provide information about any of these areas. For example, if a student expresses interest in a particular occupation, the counselor can refer to the matrix row labeled "occupation," which will provide considerable information about a specific occupation. By following the sequence of numbers and consulting the data sources listed in each box, the counselor and student can make an organized analysis of the occupation. The numbers assist the counselor in taking a logical approach to understanding both the nature of the occupation and employment opportunities for that occupation. The step-by-step approach to using LMI, beginning with any of the counseling decision areas, has been outlined in figure 5-6.

Figure 5-5
LMI Data Bank

DATA
SOURCE
LETTER   DATA SOURCE

CLASSIFICATION SYSTEMS

A.   Standard Industrial Classification Manual (SIC)
B.   Dictionary of Occupational Titles (DOT)
C.   Selected Characteristics of DOT Occupations
D.   Standard Occupational Classification Manual (SOC)
E.   Vocational Preparation and Occupations (VPO)
F.   Census Bureau Classified Index of Industries and
      Occupations

NATIONAL SOURCES

G.   Guide for Occupational Exploration (GOE)
H.   Occupational Outlook Handbook (OOH)
I.   Occupational Outlook Quarterly
J.   Exploring Careers
K.   Occupational Projections and Training Data
L.   U.S. Industrial Outlook Handbook
M.   BLS Area/Industry Wage Surveys
N.   County Business Patterns (CBP)
O.   Job Openings Bulletin Listing
P.   National Industry/Occupation Employment Matrix
      Vol. I (I/O Matrix)
Q.   National Industry/Occupation Employment Matrix
      Vol. II (Inverted Matrix)

LOCAL SOURCES

R.   State Occupational Employment Statistics I/O Matrix
      (OES I/O Matrix)
S.   OES Industry/Occupation Employment Projections
T.   ES-202 Employment Compensation and Wages Data
U.   Monthly LMI Newsletter

Figure 5-6

START WITH AN OCCUPATION

1. Select and identify occupational title.
2. Research occupational description and identify numerical code.
3. Determine the industries which employ the selected occupation and occupational concentrations in each industry.
4. Identify industry title, description, and numerical code.
5. Review the size and structure of the industrial base in local labor market to assess job opportunity.
6. Examine job openings by occupation.
7. Examine projected occupational employment opportunities.
8. Examine occupational preparation and training requirements.
9. Identify related occupations.
10. Examine occupational wage rates.
11. Examine advancement opportunity and career ladder.
12. Identify client interest areas for cross-referencing.

START WITH AN INDUSTRY

1. Select and identify industry name.
2. Research industry definition and identify numerical code.
3. Review the size and structure of the industrial base in the local labor market to assess job opportunity.
4. Determine the occupations which are employed in the selected industry and the occupational staffing pattern of the industry.
5. Select an occupational title.
6. Research occupational description and identify numerical code.
7. Examine job openings by occupation.
8. Examine projected occupational employment opportunities.
9. Examine occupation preparations and training requirements.
10. Identify related occupations.
11. Examine occupational wage rates.
12. Examine advancement opportunity and career ladder.
13. Identify client interest areas for alternate approach to exploring occupational options.

START WITH A CLIENT INTEREST AREA

1. Identify client interest area through testing or student-counselor interview process.
2. Select and identify occupational title.
3. Research occupational description and identify numerical code.
4. Determine the industries which employ the selected occupation and occupational concentrations in each industry.
5. Identify industry title, description, and numerical code.
6. Review the size and structure of the industrial base in the local labor market to assess job opportunity.
7. Examine job openings by occupation.
8. Examine projected occupational employment opportunities.
9. Examine occupational preparation and training requirements.
10. Identify related occupations.
11. Examine occupational wage rates.
12. Examine advancement opportunity and career ladder.

Conclusion

Applications of the LMI decisionmaking process matrix should greatly simplify the task of using LMI in the career-exploration process. As with most analytical tools, this matrix is designed to be flexible and adaptive to the uses of each counselor. It may be expanded to include more types of information or to include a greater number of LMI data sources. Use of the concept of the Circle of Decisions and the process provided by the LMI Decisionmaking Matrix should make the incorporation of LMI to enhance the career counseling function more practical and enlightening.

Selected Chapter Bibliography

A Counselor's Guide to Occupational Information. U.S. Department of Labor, Bureau of Labor Statistics, Washington, July 1980.

Baer, Max F. *Occupational Information, Its Nature and Use.* Chicago: Science Research Associates, 1951.

Bortz, Richard E. *Handbook for Developing Occupational Curricula.* Boston: Allyn and Bacon, 1981.

Campbell, Robert E. *Career Guidance: Handbook of Methods.* Columbus, OH: Charles Merrill, 1973.

Career and Labor Market Information: Key to Improved Individual Decision Making. U.S. Department of Labor, Employment and Training Administration, Washington, 1980.

Dictionary of Occupational Titles, Fourth Edition. Employment and Training Administration, U.S. Department of Labor, Washington, 1977.

Eschenmann, K. Kurt and Betty Heath. "Placing the Vocational Education Student." *Occupational Outlook Quarterly* (Spring 1982).

Feingold, Norman S. *Counseling for Careers in the 80's.* Garrett Park, MD: Garrett Park Press, 1979.

Ginzberg, Eli. *The Development of Human Resources.* New York: McGraw-Hill, 1966.

Guide for Occupational Exploration. Employment and Training Administration, U.S. Department of Labor, Washington, 1979.

The High School Student in the Working World: A Handbook for Counselors. Austin: Texas Education Agency, 1981.

Hoppock, Robert. *Occupational Information: Where to Get It and How to Use It in Counseling and in Teaching.* New York: McGraw-Hill, 1967.

Improved Career Decision-Making Through the Use of Labor Market Information. Employment and Training Administration, U.S. Department of Labor (undated).

Isaacson, Lee E. *Career Information in Counseling and Teaching.* Boston: Allyn and Bacon, 1977.

Kirk, Barbara Ann. *Occupational Information in Counseling: Use and Classification.* Palo Alto, CA: Consulting Psychologists Press, 1964.

McKee, William L. and Richard C. Froeschle. "Labor Market Information and Career Planning for Business Education." *Journal of Business Education* (March 1984).

Miller, Ann R., et al. *Work, Jobs and Occupations.* Washington: National Academy Press, 1980.

Occupational Outlook Handbook. Bureau of Labor Statistics, U.S. Department of Labor, Washington, 1982-3.

Occupational Projections and Training Data. Bureau of Labor Statistics, U.S. Department of Labor, Washington, 1982.

Sinick, Daniel. *Occupational Information and Guidance.* Boston: Houghton Mifflin, 1970.

Standard Occupational Classification Manual. Office of Federal Statistical Policy and Standards, U.S. Department of Commerce, Washington, 1980.

Walker, Michael J. "Guide for Occupational Exploration." *Occupational Outlook Quarterly* (Spring 1980).

Chapter 6
Summary and Conclusion

Uses of Labor Market Information

Labor market information (LMI) encompasses labor force information, occupational information, and information on where and how to find a job. One element of LMI—an indication of jobs currently available and those that are expected to become open in the future, including their wage rates and educational, training, and experience requirements—is essential for the critical decisions made by job seekers, private and public sector managers, and operators of employment and training programs. Major uses of labor market information include the following:

(1) *Policy decisions.* Information about industrial and occupational employment alerts community decision-makers to emerging problem areas and helps pinpoint alternative courses of action. LMI assists the policymaker in choosing among alternative policies and programs.

(2) *Planning.* Information on employment and job openings helps identify current and future job needs that require specific education and training. LMI assists in evaluating the need for existing training programs and the need for new training based on the expected demand for workers in various job categories.

127

(3) *Curriculum development.* Analysis of the occupational characteristics and hiring requirements of various job opportunities assists educators in identifying and developing a training curriculum. Both growing industries and technological improvements alter the nature of employers' skill requirements. By monitoring the educational and vocational preparation requirements of current and projected job opportunities, educators acquire the information necessary to adapt program content to meet the needs of a changing labor market.

(4) *Career counseling.* Information on occupational characteristics and trends are basic tools for guidance counselors and students making education and career decisions. Knowing the jobs expected to be available and their hiring requirements assists students and those undergoing career transitions in making realistic career choices.

(5) *Job development and placement.* Labor market information is used to identify the industries where employment in particular occupations is concentrated and also the industries where job openings occur. With data on specific employing establishments, job developers and placement personnel can identify those employers likely to need workers in certain occupational categories. Identifying employers can help structure an employer contact program to solicit openings for qualified job applicants.

(6) *Job search activities.* Information on job openings and job search techniques helps job seekers identify employers and industries in which their skills are in demand and helps job seekers obtain appropriate positions.

(7) *Job Training Partnership Act Applications.* This legislation, passed late in 1982 by the U.S. Congress, officially recognizes labor market information (LMI) as an indispensable component of the employment and training system. In particular, the Job Training Partnership Act's (JTPA's) emphasis on the delivery of *local* employment and training services to fulfill its paramount objective of preparing people for work relies on LMI for the following uses: program planning and evaluation, job placement, job development, job search assistance, employability development, vocational counseling, economic analysis, economic development, resource allocation, and participant eligibility determination. The concepts and techniques presented in this monograph are directly applicable to these functions, with the exception of program evaluation and participant eligibility determination which are not covered here.

The information presented in the industry and occupational analysis sections leads to the identification of target occupations in local service delivery areas. This approach can easily be performed at the county level or for an aggregation of counties. In fact, JTPA program planners will find that the applications developed here are purposely in the order of application that planners should follow in their master planning exercise.

Conclusions

This monograph concentrates on the process of identifying current and future job openings and their specific educational and training requirements.

Selecting target jobs basically involves the identification of those occupations which exhibit acceptable terms of employment (e.g., long-term stability, promotion opportunities, etc.) and working conditions, and which also possess a high potential for job placement. Ideally, target jobs would be "good" jobs in which there exist unfilled job openings and an excess demand. Complete measures of either existing or future vacancies are unavailable, however. Hence, the selection process involves melding fragments of information into a realistic judgment of where job openings can be expected. What job opportunities are available? What occupations are in demand? In what areas is there a high potential for job placement? What are the hiring qualifications? The quality of the final decision depends upon having adequate information to answer these questions to make an informed judgment of where the best employment potential exists.

Information on job openings is of prime value to the program planner and job seeker. Openings occur through (1) employment growth and (2) a need to replace workers lost through separation from the labor force or through transfers out of an occupation. Employment and job openings among occupations depend, in part, upon employment levels within particular industries. While the available sources of LMI do not supply the precise number and characteristics of total job openings, many sources are available that can be used to narrow the labor market and focus on the industries, occupations, and employers where openings can reasonably be expected to occur. A systematic, yet uncomplicated, analytical process for identifying job opportunities entails a careful study of local employment trends and projections—first at the industry level and then by occupation. Through this process, existing LMI such as data from Job Bank or ESARS, can be used to identify potential job openings among employers.

There is no substitute for personal contact with employers in gathering information on a firm's hiring requirements. While the majority of training takes place on the job, through direct employer contact the analyst can identify the minimum qualifications necessary for the firm's entry- and mid-level positions. Ideally, by selecting those occupations demonstrating the greatest employment potential and combining that knowledge with an understanding of the qualities of those occupations, job search and training program planning, as well as career guidance and business decisions, can become more effective. In addition, better job matches will result in reduced labor turnover and enhanced productivity, which are benefits that accrue to society at large.

Appendix

Appendix 1
Fundamental Concepts

Labor Market Information

Labor market information (LMI) is any information that enhances one's understanding of the structure and functions of a labor market. With such a broad view, understandably, there are many federal, state, and local agencies responsible for providing data and assistance in the process of researching local communities and identifying job opportunities. Many of the data items currently available were first produced in response to a specific user need. Consequently, because of the diversity and quantity of these items, obtaining and using LMI can often be a frustrating task if a systematic process is not followed.

Within the U.S. Department of Labor, the LMI network consists primarily of an interagency working arrangement between the Employment and Training Administration (ETA), the Bureau of Labor Statistics (BLS), and each state employment security agency (ES). ETA plays a major role in planning and funding LMI materials, and the BLS provides the technical support and guidance in carrying out the cooperative statistical programs (employment, unemployment, occupational projections, labor turnover statistics, and employment and wages in firms covered by the unemployment insurance program). Each of these agencies is involved to some extent in LMI production and distribution. At the local level, however, the ES has primary responsibility for making LMI available.

Labor Force Components

Household labor force data, covering employment and unemployment as well as the characteristics of workers and

135

136

their jobs, are obtained from: (1) the decennial census (the census labor force data actually are collected from a sample of the population), and (2) the Current Population Survey (CPS), a program of personal interviews conducted *monthly* by the Bureau of the Census for the Bureau of Labor Statistics (BLS). The CPS sample consists of about 60,000 households selected to represent the U.S. population 16 years of age and older. Effective January 1983, the BLS published, in addition to the traditional *civilian* labor force series, a new labor force series that includes armed forces personnel stationed in the U.S.

An *establishment* employment series, covering employment, hours, and earnings data, is compiled, separately from the CPS, from payroll records reported monthly on a voluntary basis to the BLS and cooperating ESs by 177,000 establishments representing all industries except agriculture. Because of sample coverage and definitional differences, the monthly household and establishment employment series are not directly comparable.

Household Survey Definitions

Employed persons are (1) those who worked for pay any time during the week which includes the 12th day of the month or who worked unpaid for 15 hours or more in a family-operated enterprise and (2) those who were temporarily absent from their regular jobs because of illness, vacation, industrial dispute, or similar reasons. A person working at more than one job is counted only in the job at which he or she worked the greatest number of hours.

Unemployed persons are those who did not work during the survey week, but were available for work except for temporary illness and had looked for jobs within the preceding four weeks. Persons who did not look for work because they were on layoff or waiting to start new jobs within the next 30 days are also counted among the unemployed. The unemployment rate represents the number unemployed as a percent of the civilian labor force.

The *civilian labor force* consists of all employed or unemployed persons in the civilian noninstitutional population; the total labor force includes military personnel. Persons not in the labor force are those not classified as employed or unemployed; this group includes persons retired, those engaged in their own housework, those not working while attending school, those unable to work because of long term illness, those discouraged from seeking work because of personal or job market factors, and those who are voluntarily idle. The noninstitutional population comprises all persons 16 years of age and older who are not inmates of penal or mental institutions, sanitariums, or homes for the aged, infirm, or needy.

Regional Change

Extensive research on the process of regional and urban economic development has been conducted over the time period since World War II. While the quantity of technical analysis continues to be considerable, the research is by no means in agreement on what specifically causes regional growth or decline to occur in a particular geographic setting. Recent studies, however, have tended to identify an amorphous process at work, whereby economic growth is generated by the interaction of a number of economic variables rather than through any single factor in isolation. This section identifies and discusses some of the more important concepts and relationships pertaining to regional economic development, with the overriding objective of providing the reader with a sufficient framework for studying the analytical applications that are performed in subsequent sections.

Measures of Regional Growth

Before proceeding to a discussion of how regions develop, it is first necessary to address the notion of how economic progress is measured. Economic progress, from a traditional perspective, is measured by changes in any one or a combination of the factors of population (or employment), income levels, production, or structural changes in the economic environment. Population as an economic growth indicator is, by itself, an ambiguous measure of economic progress. Employment, alternatively, is more directly tied to the market place and, thus, provides a clearer and more responsive measure of economic development. Since employment does not exist in the absence of consumer demand, however, employment is certainly tied to the size and composition of a local area's population.

Historically, rates of population and employment change have differed considerably among areas of the U.S. Since 1860, for example, the earliest settled states along the eastern seaboard have grown at rates well below the national average, while the far west has grown at above averages rates since the early 1800s. While these divergent growth paths are to be expected as the frontier was conquered, the more contemporary phenomenon has been for population growth to become more equalized across areas. Employment growth, on an historical basis, has tended to move coincidentally with population growth, thus leading many observers to conclude either that employment shifts cause population migration or vice versa.

Income

Much attention has also been directed to persistently lower per capita income levels in the south relative to the rest of the U.S. and, particularly, the north. However, since 1880, and even more so after 1960, there has persisted a general trend toward convergence of per capita income levels among regions of the country. The "sunbelt phenomenon," in this sense, has accelerated the movement toward regional income equality rather than inequality. Because of cost-of-living differences as well as other factors, there currently exists no hard evidence to support the claim that northern employers' real labor costs exceed those of their southern counterparts nor that southern workers are economically better situated than workers in the north.

Structural changes

Although more difficult to quantify precisely at times, improvements in educational levels and literacy, technological advancements, and improved utilization of productive resources also point to regional economic growth. As indicated earlier in terms of income and population trends, there exists substantial evidence to suggest that these factors are also becoming more equalized across the U.S.

What causes growth?

While there is no clear-cut answer to this question, several factors are recognized to have considerable impact on the issue. Needless to say, however, serious disagreement still persists regarding the relative importance of any one variable. Similar to the more recent debate among supplyside and Keynesian economists, regional analysts have broken camp over which factor of supply or demand is more important in its effects on regional growth. Very similar arguments are heard in the debate over the "push" and "pull" element of population migration. Thus, the argument centers on the causal relationship between regional population and regional employment growth. Do people follow jobs, or do jobs follow people?

In terms of jobs following people, considerable evidence can be gathered to show that population growth is the most significant variable in explaining employment. Similar studies emphasize a number of locational influences, including labor, other resources, climate, markets, and agglomeration (the tendency for firms in the same industry to cluster around one another for efficiency purposes).

Alternatively, many authors are committed to their assertion that people follow jobs. Such factors as the availability of space encourage the relocation of industrial plants and thereby encourage the migration of workers to the expanding areas. Thus, prospective employment determines the nature and direction of migration.

It has only been recently, however, that attention has been directed to reconciling the opposing views on the causal relationship between employment growth and migration. Several studies have validated the mutual interdependence and causality of migration and employment growth. While it is argued that, at least in the original step in the sequence, migration of the labor force is responsive to job opportunities, it follows that the migrants themselves end up influencing both the supply of, and demand for, local labor. The economy, as well as employment, therefore, grows most rapidly in those areas that have attracted migrants. Areas of declining population due to out-migration, alternatively, will have the least economic growth.

Labor Turnover

A careful consideration of turnover is particularly important, although difficult to approach quantitatively, in any analysis of employment opportunity. Since the process of workers leaving jobs (commonly referred to as separations) is normally a larger source of job openings than employment expansion through growth, understanding labor turnover and observing the patterns of worker separation from employment is a critical part of identifying job openings. Unfortunately, the Bureau of Labor Statistics' survey of turnover in manufacturing industries, the Labor Turnover

Statistics Program, was terminated in December 1981 due to funding cutbacks. Other more sophisticated data sources on new hires by industries continue to emerge.

Strictly defined, *labor turnover* refers to the gross movement of workers into and out of employment with individual establishments. Most often, when workers separate or move out of employment, openings are generated. For measurement purposes, the Bureau of Labor Statistics has developed technical definitions of these worker transactions. According to the BLS, turnover consists of accessions and separations, which are broken into component parts according to the following:

Accessions = New Hires + Recalls + Other Accessions
Separations = Quits + Layoffs + Other Separations

Separations are terminations of employment of persons who have quit or been taken off the rolls for reasons such as layoff, discharge, retirement, death, military service, physical disability, transfers to other establishments, etc.

Quits are terminations of employment initiated by employees for any reason except retirement, transfer to another establishment of the same firm, or service in the Armed Forces. Included as quits are persons who failed to report after being hired and unauthorized absences which have lasted more than seven consecutive days.

Layoffs are suspensions from pay status initiated by the employer without prejudice to the worker, for reasons such as lack of orders, model changeover, termination of seasonal or temporary employment, inventory taking, introduction of labor saving devices, plant breakdown, or shortage of materials.

Discharges are terminations of employment initiated by the employer for such reasons as incompetence, violation of rules, dishonesty, laziness, absenteeism, insubordination, failure to pass probationary period, etc.

Other separations include terminations of employment for military duty lasting more than thirty days, retirement, death, permanent disability, failure to meet the physical standards required, and transfers of employees to another establishment of the company.

Accessions are all permanent and temporary additions to the employment roll, whether of new or rehired employees. Transfers from another establishment of the same company also are counted as accessions.

New hires are permanent and temporary additions to the employment roll of persons who have never before been employed by the establishment and former employees rehired although not specifically recalled by the employer. This category excludes transfers from other establishments of the same company and employees returning from military service or unpaid leaves of absence.

Recalls are permanent or temporary additions to the employment roll of persons specifically recalled to a job in the same establishment of the company following a period of layoff lasting more than seven consecutive days.

Other accessions include all additions to the employment roll other than new hires and recalls.

Turnover Analysis

In the analysis of job opportunities, especially in identifying where job openings are likely to occur, it must be noted that large firms normally have lower turnover rates than small firms. It has been estimated for California, where turnover is measured in a representative sample, that turnover rates in firms with less than 100 employees are more than twice as high as in firms with more than 1,000 employees.

While the causes of this phenomenon are not precisely documented, it can be argued that the heavy representation of part-time students and other secondary workers in small eating and drinking establishments, as well as in other wholesale and retail firms, tends to magnify turnover in small firms.

Even though turnover in small firms may be at twice the rate of much larger firms, it is obvious that the total number of job openings created by turnover in a firm of 1,000 employees will be about five times as many as the openings due to turnover in a firm of 100. Stated simply, most of the job openings due to turnover will occur in firms and industries where most of the jobs are located, although turnover rates may be higher in smaller firms.

Accessions

New hire and other worker accession data provide some of the most direct indications of potential job openings among various industries. Information on new hires, the new hire rate, and worker accessions are provided by the Department of Labor's Employment Service Potential (ESP) and Employer Information Systems (EIS) Projects (see chapter 1).

The ESP and EIS projects utilize State Employment Security Agency (ES) unemployment compensation insurance records, submitted by almost every employer, to track individual employees by industry and employer and to compute new hire data. Both the ESP and EIS programs are new, however, and data are generally available only for major and 2-digit (SIC) industries for the United States, as well as the major industrial levels within each state. Some pilot states have operational systems that provide detailed new hire rates for the state as well as substate areas. In most states, though, ESP and EIS information is limited so the analysis must be built around national data as indicators of local industry new hires. Since information on new hires is an important indicator of job openings potential, but, because current detailed data are unavailable for most states and local areas, it is not the only factor that should be considered.

Uses of Labor Turnover Data

Information on turnover is critical in understanding the operation of labor markets and the aggregate economy, as well as in comparing the performance of individual firms. Economists for some time have used layoff and quit rates, which move in opposite directions at any point in the business cycle, as leading economic indicators of the direction in which the economy is heading. Since layoffs and quits are cyclically sensitive, information on the behavior of these factors aids in predicting the turning points of economic trends.

It is significant, moreover, to note that over the past thirty years there has persisted a downward trend in layoff rates, reflecting the increased costs to the firm of replacing workers who fail to return from layoff as well as evidencing, perhaps, the impact of other mechanisms such as collective bargaining contracts. Quit rates, alternatively, give evidence of the changing availability of job openings. Workers most often quit either to (1) look for another job or (2) leave the labor force. Changes in the quit rate, consequently, normally reflect changes in the availability of job openings, since labor force withdrawals are generally stable over one- or two-year periods.

Firms can make use of labor turnover information in order to gauge the performance of their overall operations, or even of their individual plants, in comparison to the industry as a whole. If turnover in certain plants or among certain employee classifications is found to be comparatively excessive, management may need to take steps aimed at reducing particular types of turnover.

Appendix 2
Sources of Labor Market Information

Checklist of Selected Labor Market
Information Publications

1. ____ **Dictionary of Occupational Titles (DOT),** Fourth edition . . . Provides detailed descriptions for 20,000 occupations including related job titles and job tasks. U.S. Department of Labor (DOL)/U.S. Employment Service (USES). Available through the Government Printing Office (GPO). Stock No. 029-013-00079-9

2. ____ **Selected Characteristics of Occupations Defined in the DOT** . . . Provides supplemental information concerning physical demands, environmental conditions and restrictions, and training time for DOT defined occupations. U.S. DOL/USES. Available through the GPO. Stock No. 1980 0-301-764

3. ____ **Standard Occupational Classification Manual (SOC) 1980** . . . Provides a coding system for classifying occupational information by job duties with groups to identify related occupational clusters. U.S. Department of Commerce. Available through the GPO. Stock No. 1980 0-332-946

4. ____ **Standard Industrial Classification (SIC) Manual 1972** . . . Provides a coding system for classifying, collecting, and disseminating data by industry grouping. Office of Management and Budget (OMB). Available through the GPO. Stock No. 1981 0-359-712:QL 3

5. ____ **Occupational Outlook Handbook (OOH)** . . . Contains detailed information for 250 selected occupations including narratives on the nature of work, training and qualifications, job outlook and earnings. U.S. DOL/Bureau of Labor Statistics. Available through the GPO. Bulletin 2200

6. ____ **Exploring Careers** . . . Career education resource providing career and world-of-work awareness through stories, basic job facts and career games. U.S. DOL/Bureau of Labor Statistics. Available through the GPO. Bulletin 2001-(1-15)

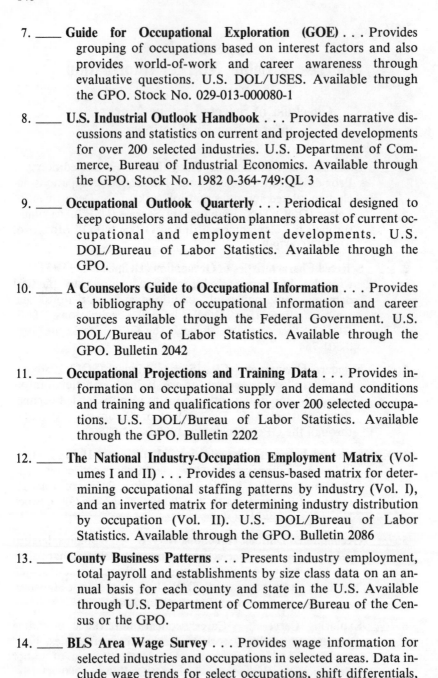

7. ____ **Guide for Occupational Exploration (GOE)** . . . Provides grouping of occupations based on interest factors and also provides world-of-work and career awareness through evaluative questions. U.S. DOL/USES. Available through the GPO. Stock No. 029-013-000080-1

8. ____ **U.S. Industrial Outlook Handbook** . . . Provides narrative discussions and statistics on current and projected developments for over 200 selected industries. U.S. Department of Commerce, Bureau of Industrial Economics. Available through the GPO. Stock No. 1982 0-364-749:QL 3

9. ____ **Occupational Outlook Quarterly** . . . Periodical designed to keep counselors and education planners abreast of current occupational and employment developments. U.S. DOL/Bureau of Labor Statistics. Available through the GPO.

10. ____ **A Counselors Guide to Occupational Information** . . . Provides a bibliography of occupational information and career sources available through the Federal Government. U.S. DOL/Bureau of Labor Statistics. Available through the GPO. Bulletin 2042

11. ____ **Occupational Projections and Training Data** . . . Provides information on occupational supply and demand conditions and training and qualifications for over 200 selected occupations. U.S. DOL/Bureau of Labor Statistics. Available through the GPO. Bulletin 2202

12. ____ **The National Industry-Occupation Employment Matrix** (Volumes I and II) . . . Provides a census-based matrix for determining occupational staffing patterns by industry (Vol. I), and an inverted matrix for determining industry distribution by occupation (Vol. II). U.S. DOL/Bureau of Labor Statistics. Available through the GPO. Bulletin 2086

13. ____ **County Business Patterns** . . . Presents industry employment, total payroll and establishments by size class data on an annual basis for each county and state in the U.S. Available through U.S. Department of Commerce/Bureau of the Census or the GPO.

14. ____ **BLS Area Wage Survey** . . . Provides wage information for selected industries and occupations in selected areas. Data include wage trends for select occupations, shift differentials,

benefits and straight time earnings. Available from the U.S. DOL, Bureau of Labor Statistics or the GPO.

15. ____ **EEOC Report of Minorities and Women in Private Industry** . . . Provides the makeup of industry workforce by sex and by race/ethnic categories for each state and MSA with population of one million or more. Includes employment by major occupational category, participation rate and occupational percent distribution. Available through the U.S. Equal Employment Opportunity Commission.

16. ____ **Vocational Preparation and Occupations (VPO)** . . . Crosswalk volume which allows for comparison of occupational information across several occupational coding structures. Included are the OES survey and matrix codes, DOT, SOC, 1980 Census and CIP. Available in print or on tape through the National Occupational Information Coordinating Committee (NOICC).

17. ____ **OES Industry Staffing Patterns** (actual title varies) . . . Occupational distribution of employment generally by 3-digit SIC category. Identifies which occupations are employed in which industries and their relative concentrations. Available through the Employment Service, in each state.

18. ____ **OES State and Area Projections** (actual title varies) . . . Industry and occupation, employment projections for the state and metro areas. Available through the Employment Service in each state.

19. ____ **Covered Wages and Employment** (ES-202) . . . Industry employment data taken from employer UI tax records. Available at the county level in varying levels of industry detail. Available through the Employment Service in each state.

20. ____ **Monthly Labor Market Information Newsletter** (actual title varies) . . . Monthly newsletter which monitors changes in total employment, labor force, unemployment, hours and earnings and other selected data for the state and some substate areas. Available through the Employment Service in each state.

21. ____ **Characteristics of the Insured Unemployed** (ES-203) . . . Program monitors characteristics of persons on the UI roles including former industry and occupation attachment, sex, age

and weeks of unemployment duration. Available through the Employment Service (not available in every state).

22. ____ **1980 Census of Population and Housing (Detailed Population Characteristics)** ... Decennial census of the population provides complete counts of the population, employment, income and detailed characteristics by age, sex, race and household status. Data available for states, metro areas, counties, incorporated places and census tracts. Available on tape or hard copy from the U.S. Bureau of the Census or various state data management centers.

Mailing Address:
Superintendent of Documents
U.S. Government Printing Office
Washington, DC 20402

NOTE: Most Bureau of Labor Statistics documents are also available at BLS Regional Offices.

Table A2-1
Sources of Labor Market Information

DATA ELEMENT	GEOGRAPHIC COVERAGE	TIMING	SOURCE / INDUSTRIAL DATA	AGENCY
Total Labor Force	SDA/County County MSA/State	Monthly Decennial Monthly	LAUS estimate 1980 Census of Population Report 3 Table 7 Monthly LMI Newsletter	ES ES ES
Total Employment	SDA/County MSA/State	Monthly Monthly	LAUS estimates Monthly LMI Newsletter	ES ES
1. By Industry	State/ Major LMAs	Monthly	Current Employment Statistics (CES) (also referred to as BLS-790)	ES
	State/SDA/ County	Quarterly	ES-202 (occasional disclosure)	ES
	County/State/ MSA	Annual	County Business Patterns	Dept. of Commerce
2. By Occupation	State/MSA	Periodic	Occupational Employment Statistics Survey	ES
	County	Decennial	1980 Census of Population Report 3 Table 12	Bureau of Census
Occupational Wage	MSA	Quarterly	ESARS-Table 7B (may not be available for all MSAs)	ES
	MSA/Local Office	Monthly	Job Bank	ES
	MSA	Annual	Area Wage Survey (for selected MSAs and selected occupations only)	BLS

ES - Employment Service
LAUS-Local Area Unemployment Statistics Program
BLS - Bureau of Labor Statistics

MSA - Metropolitan Statistical Area
SDA - Service Delivery Area (Job Training Partnership Act)
Local Office - Employment Service

Table A-1 (continued)

DATA ELEMENT	GEOGRAPHIC COVERAGE	TIMING	SOURCE INDUSTRIAL DATA	AGENCY
Total Industrial Wages/Payroll	County	Quarterly	ES-202	ES
Industrial Wage Rates	County/MSA	Annual	County Business Patterns	Dept. of Commerce
	State/ Major LMAs	Monthly	Current Employment Statistics (790 program) published in Employment and Earnings and in Monthly LMI Newsletters	ES
	National/ Regional/ State/ MSA	5-year Recurring cycle Monthly	Industry Wage Surveys	BLS
Labor Turnover	Selected States/MSA	Quarterly	Employment Service Potential (ESP)	ES
New Hire Rates	National	1974 and 1978	1% Social Security Sample	University of Michigan
Projected Occupational Demand	MSA/State	Periodic	Occupational Projections to 1985 and 1990 from the OES survey (includes annual average openings by expansion and replacement.	ES
				Also, Trade Associations, Vocational Education, other planning agencies, etc.

DATA ELEMENT	GEOGRAPHIC COVERAGE	TIMING	SOURCE INDUSTRIAL DATA	AGENCY
Number of Unemployed	MSA/County	Monthly	LAUS estimates	ES
Unemployment Rate	State/MSA/County	Monthly	LAUS estimates monthly newsletter	ES
*Job Openings by Industry	MSA/County	Monthly	ESARS-Table 12 (may not be available for all MSAs)	ES
*Job Openings by Occupation	MSA/County	Quarterly	ESARS-Table 96B (may not be available for all MSAs)	ES
	MSA/City	Daily	Want Ads	Newspapers
Unfilled Job Openings	MSA	Quarterly	ESARS-Table 96B (may not be available for all MSAs)	MSA
	MSA/City	Daily	Want Ads	Newspapers
Employers in Growing Industries and Occupations	MSA/County/SDA	Varying	Based on review of available industry-related LMI	Various Agencies
Directory of Employers	MSA/County	Varying	Major Market Listing	ES
	MSA/County/State	Varying	Directory of Manufacturers	Public or University Library
	County	Annual	Million Dollar Directory, vol. 1 Middle Market Directory, vol. 2	Dun & Bradstreet Inc.
	County/City	Annual	Chamber of Commerce Listing of Local Manufacturers Membership Directory	Chamber of Commerce

*Refers only to openings listed through the Employment Service.

Table A-1 (continued)

DATA ELEMENT	GEOGRAPHIC COVERAGE	TIMING	SOURCE DEMOGRAPHIC DATA	AGENCY
Total Population Characteristics	County/SDA	1980	Lawrence Berkeley Laboratory (LBL) ETA/Census Report 3	ETA/LBL
	County/Census Tract	Decennial (1980)	Census of Population	Bureau of the Census
	County/City	Annual	Current Population Reports (P-25)	Bureau of the Census
				ES
Age Distribution	State/MSA/County	Decennial	1980 Census of Population Report 3 Table II	Bureau of the Census
	State/Selected MDS	One-time (1976)	Survey of Income and Education	ES-HHS-Census
Sex	State/MSA	Annual	EEOC Report of Minorities and Women	EEOC
	State/Selected MSA	One-time (1976)	Survey of Income and Education	ES-HHS-Census
	County	Monthly	Affirmative Action Data	ES
	Varied	Decennial (1980)	Census of Population: General, Social and Economic Characteristics Report 3 Table I, III	Bureau of the Census

ETA/LBL - Lawrence Berkeley Laboratory under contract to the Employment and Training Administration, U.S. Department of Labor

SDA - Service Delivery Area designated under the Jobs Training Partnership Act
EEOC - Equal Employment Opportunity Commission
HHS - U.S. Department of Health and Human Services

DATA ELEMENT	GEOGRAPHIC COVERAGE	TIMING	SOURCE DEMOGRAPHIC DATA	AGENCY
Total Population Characteristics	State/MSA	Annual	EEOC Report on Minorities and Women	EEOC
Race/Ethnic Group	MSA/County/ State Selected MSA	Decennial One-time (1976)	1980 Census of Population Report 3, Survey of Income and Education	Bureau of the Census ES-HHS-Census
	County	Monthly	Affirmative Action Data	ES
Low Income Adults	State/County	Annual (1980)	Public Assistance Recipients in SMSA	Health and Human Services
	State/ Selected MSA	One-time (1976)	Survey of Income and Education	ES-HHS-Census
	Varied	1980	ETA/Census Report #2 Report 3, Table 19	ETA/LBL Bureau of the Census
Veterans	State/County	Biennially	State and County Veteran Population	Veterans Administration
	State/County	Decennial	1980 Census of Population Report 3, Table IV	Bureau of the Census, ES-HHS-Census
Economically Disadvantaged	SDA/State	One-time	State Planning Information	ES
	Varied	1980	ETA Report #2 and E3 Table IXX	ETA/LBL

EEOC - Equal Employment Opportunity Commission

Table A-1 (continued)

DATA ELEMENT	GEOGRAPHIC COVERAGE	TIMING	SOURCE DEMOGRAPHIC DATA	AGENCY
Educational Attainment	MSA	1980	Census-Tables 120, 125 and 130	Bureau of the Census
Total Population Characteristics	Varied	1980	ETA/Census Report #3, Table VI	ETA/BL
Birth Rates	MSA/SDA	Annual	(Title of publication varies)	State Health Department, Bureau of Vital Statistics
Death Rates	MSA/SDA	Annual	(Title of publication varies)	State Health Department, Bureau of Vital Statistics
	National	Annual	Mortality Tables	Major Life Insurance Companies
Total Migration	County	1975-80	Net Migration of the Population 1975-80, by Age, Sex, and Color	Census Bureau
Migration Rate	County	1975-80	Net Migration of the Population 1975-80, by Age, Sex, and Color	Census Bureau
	County	Annual	Current Population Report Series	Census
Per Capita Income	MSA/County	Annual	Per Capita Personal Income in MSAs and Counties in Selected Years (CPR P-25)	Bureau of Economic Analysis (BEA) (should be available from ES)
Total Personal Income	County/City MSA/County	Periodic Annual	Current Population Reports Total Personal Income in MSAs and Counties in Selected Years	Bureau of the Census BEA (should be available from ES)

DATA ELEMENT	GEOGRAPHIC COVERAGE	TIMING	SOURCE DEMOGRAPHIC DATA	AGENCY
Total Unemployed	MSA/County	Monthly	LAUS estimates	ES
	State/MSA	Monthly	Monthly LMI Newsletter	ES
1. By Age	Statewide	Annual	ES-203* and ESARS Table 08, 93	ES
2. By Sex	Statewide	Annual	Es-203* and ESARS Table 08, 93	ES
3. By Race/Ethnic Group	County	Decennial	1980 Census of Population Reports, Table VIII	Bureau of the Census
4. By Industry	National	Monthly	Employment and Earnings, Table A-18	BLS
	State/Selected MSA	Monthly	ES-203*	ES
5. By Occupation	National	Monthly	Employment and Earnings, Table A-18	BLS
	MSA	Monthly	ES-203* For states and selected MSAs and on a sample basis only	ES
Reasons for Unemployment and Underemployment	MSA National	Monthly Monthly	ESARS Employment and Earnings, Tables A-12, A-13, A-15	ES BLS

*Indicates a data source which may no longer be available in many states.

Table A-1 (continued)

DATA ELEMENT	GEOGRAPHIC COVERAGE	TIMING	SOURCE DEMOGRAPHIC DATA	AGENCY
Duration of Unemployment	National	Monthly	Employment and Earnings, Tables A-13 A-14, A-17, A-18	BLS
	MSA	Monthly	ES-203* For states and selected MSAs and on a sample basis only	ES
Educational Attainment	County	Monthly	ESARS-Table 93, ES Applicants	ES
School Dropouts	County	Annual	(Title of publication varies)	Check with State Department of Education or local school board
Welfare Recipients	State/County	Annual	Public Assistance Recipients	Health and Human Services
	County	Monthly	ESARS-Table 93, ES Applicants	ES
	County	Monthly	(Title of publication varies)	County Welfare Department
Food Stamp Recipients	County	Monthly	ESARS-Table 93, ES Applicants	ES
	County	Monthly	(Title of publication varies)	State or County Department of Welfare

*Indicates a data source which may no longer be available in many states.

DATA ELEMENT	GEOGRAPHIC COVERAGE	TIMING	SOURCE DEMOGRAPHIC DATA	AGENCY
Handicapped	County	Monthly	ESARS-Table 93, ES Applicants	ES
Old Age Assistance Recipients	County	Monthly	(Title of publication varies)	County Department of Welfare
Aid to the Blind	County	Monthly	(Title of publication varies)	County Department of Welfare
Aid to the Disabled	County	Monthly	(Title of publication varies)	County Department of Welfare
Apprenticeship Programs	MSA/County	Varying	Apprenticeship Program Representative	ES and State Bureau of Apprenticeship and Training
Private Vocational and Business School Graduates	MSA/County	Annual	(Title of publication varies)	State Department of Education
Community College Graduates	MSA/County	Annual	(Title of publication varies)	State Department of Education
High School Graduates	MSA/County	Annual	(Title of publication varies)	State Department of Education
Other Educational Institution Graduates	MSA/County	Annual	(Title of publication varies)	State Department of Education

Appendix 3
Industrial Evaluative Model

Introduction

Working systematically through the process model detailed in chapter 3, the analyst should be able to select several industrial sectors within the local economy which represent greater employment and job opening potential. Despite the many subtleties involved in interpreting statistical data, this process may become more quantitative by employing a statistical model. This appendix offers an example of just such a model, which consists of several labor market indicators incorporated into a weighted equation.

The nine economic indicators presented here have been chosen in an attempt to capture both the local and national dynamics of each particular industry. This process has been simplified by using the same indicators for each industry. Users should recognize that, by employing a different set of indicators for each industry, a more thorough industry-by-industry analysis would be possible. However, this model has been developed to provide a relative *comparative* analysis of each industry within the local economy. Analysts attempting to employ this or similar evaluative models may wish to select alternative indicators which they feel provide better barometers of local industry performance.

In any such weighted model, the value assigned to each indicator is, to one degree or another, a subjective reflection of the analyst's view of the local economy. Although the intuitive understanding of the analyst is invaluable in working through this process, it is important that the final synthesis of the statistical data be as objective and free from bias as possible. This weighted model approach provides a method by which the analyst may objectively rank each industry in

159

the local economy using both statistical data and his or her understanding of local economic forces.

It must be stressed that this model is designed to identify industries in the local economy with greater job opening potential on a relative basis. Its application for other purposes may limit its interpretive ability. Without denigrating the accuracy of this model, the analyst is reminded that there are limitations to its application which are inherent in any attempt at modeling. However, the authors have used this evaluative modeling technique on several occasions and found it to be extremely valuable in synthesizing the large amount of statistical data required in local economic analysis.

Background

The various economic indicators used in this model already have been presented and discussed in previous steps of the industry analytical process. For each of these variables, the appropriate data source has been identified. Table A3-1 displays the evaluative model and the weight factors applied to each variable. The variables reflect the current economic situation and historic and future trends in the local economy, as well as several measures of industrial performance. This model may be applied at any level of industrial detail desired for which data are available. It is recommended that data with a 2-digit (SIC) industrial level of detail be used because this level enjoys both adequate detail and the data are readily available. Caution must be taken, however, to compare industrial sectors at the same level of detail. Two-digit data, for example, should not be enjoined with data at the major division or 3-digit level.

Table A3-1
Industry Analysis Evaluative Model

$$\text{Industry Evaluation Quotient (IEQ)} = \begin{array}{l} .20(A) + .20(B) + .10(C) + .10(D) + .10(E) + \\ .10(F) + .10(G) + .05(H) + .05(I) \end{array}$$

- -

INDICATOR DESIGNATION	WEIGHT FACTOR	ECONOMIC INDICATOR
(A)	20%	Current level of employment (rank).
(B)	20%	Greatest absolute employment increase over an historical period (rank).
(C)	10%	Future employment projections (rank).
(D)	10%	Current level of business establishments (rank).
(E)	10%	Greatest absolute change in business establishments over an historical period (rank).
(F)	10%	Current industry job openings: (0-99)=5 points, (100-299)=4 points, (300-399)=3 points, (400-499)=2 points, (500 and above)=1 point.
(G)	10%	Potential new hires (rank). (National new hire rate x local employment.)
(H)	5%	Index of aggregate hours (rank). (National series indexing weekly hours and production workers.)
(I)	5%	Base industry status (points): if yes - 10 points, if no = 30 points.
9 variables	100%	

Economic Indicators

The most heavily weighted indicators in the model are (A) the current level of employment and (B) the greatest absolute increase in employment over an historical period. Each of these categories is weighted 20 percent. The current employment level of each industry is determined and then each is ranked, with the rank of 1 assigned to the largest industry. Even in a stagnant economy where no growth is occurring, there are job openings due to replacement needs. The degree to which these openings are refilled is best represented by the industry new hire rate. By multiplying the new hire rate by the size of the existing workforce, the number of anticipated replacements is derived. This category emphasizes, then, that the larger the existing industry workforce, the greater the potential number of new employees to be hired.

Category B, the greatest absolute increase in the level of employment over an historic period, is entered to capture underlying trends in industrial growth. Historic growth trends should also be considered in projecting where growth may develop in the future. For local areas with little or no growth in recent years, the focus will shift to those local industries which have declined the least and/or have remained prosperous at the national level. Numerical rather than percent change is used because the objective is to identify industries with the greatest number of potential job openings. Although a large percentage increase may indicate an expanding industry, it also disguises the gross number of potential openings. Still, a significant percentage increase in an industry could be added as a separate indicator should the situation warrant. As with current employment, the numerical employment change is calculated for each industry and ranked, with the industry demonstrating the greatest increase receiving the top ranking.

Category C, future projections of industry employment, introduces industrial projections of employment by industry. These projections are awarded a 10 percent weight. Greater weight might be given to projections, depending on the uncertainty of the economic and political circumstances within which local industry will be operating into the future. Despite the sophistication of these models, predicting the local economic future is an especially difficult and uncertain endeavor, and industrial projections are not regularly available at the county level. Where the county is included in an MSA, these projections may be substituted. In the event that neither county nor MSA industrial projections are available, statewide projections may be incorporated, or employment projections may be deleted altogether and the 10 percent weight factor redistributed among the other variables. The industry with the greatest absolute projected increase in employment is ranked first, with the rest of the field receiving their respective positions in the rank order.

The fourth indicator, D, is the current number of business establishments in the industry. The industry with the greatest number of establishments is ranked first, with the other industries falling in their respective places. The level of business establishments represents the number of firms that are potential locations of hiring activity. Regardless of the size of the establishment, research indicates that the more firms in an industry the greater the probability that at least some will be growing and generating job opportunities.

Similar to the rationale for the last indicator, the greatest absolute increase in business establishments over an historical period, E, is used as a surrogate for industrial prosperity and given a weight of 10 percent. If the number of business establishments in an industry has been increasing over a recent period, this is a good indication that demand for the industry's product is attracting new entrepreneurial entrants into the industry with corresponding increases in job opportunities. Alternatively, if an industry has been experiencing a decline in business establishments over a recent period, either industry demand is not strong enough to support the existing level of existing establishments, or the stronger firms are absorbing the others. Generally, a decline in establishments occurs concomitantly with a decline in job opportunities. Therefore, those industries having the greater increases in establishments are ranked first, and those units with the largest declines or smallest increases are last.

The sixth ranked indicator, F, focuses on current industry job openings. Due to data limitations, it represents those job openings (by industry) filed by employers with the local ES. Although current job openings would seem to be a valuable indicator, its efficacy is reduced due to the small share of total job openings received by the ES. Therefore, this category is given a weight factor of only 10 percent. A sliding point scale is applied to total job openings available. The data are taken from the ES Job Bank data for the most current month for which the data are available. If total available openings (TAO) are 99 or less (TAO $\leq$ 99), the industry receives 5 points, from 100-299, 4 points, and so forth according to the table. These point scores are then multiplied by the weight factor, which is 10 percent. (It is important to remember that in this model the *lower* the final score, the greater the job potential attributed to an industry. It follows that a large number of openings is a very positive sign of job activity and therefore receives the *smallest* point score.)

The seventh variable in the weighted equation is G, the rank of potential new hires within an industry. Potential new hires are calculated by multiplying national industrial new hire rates by local industry employment. The resulting number of potential industry new hires is then rank ordered by industry and the ranks subsequently multiplied by a weight factor of 10 percent. The inclusion of new hire rates and potential new hires introduces labor turnover activity, which varies by industry. A high new hire rate indicates greater hiring activity is taking place which means a greater number of potential job opportunities will arise in that industry. The estimate of new hire activity combines job openings created both through growth and replacement.

The final two variables in the equation introduce regional and national trends into the evaluative model. Because all local economies are affected by regional and national activity, the model realistically needs a measure which monitors national industrial performance. The eighth indicator, H, is an index of aggregate hours, similar to the measure produced by the Bureau of Labor Statistics. The index is based on average weekly hours worked and the number of production workers. The use of average weekly hours is a longstanding indicator of economic activity and is included here to capture national trends. These trends, within varying degrees, are representative of regional and local experiences, given an area's lead or lag sensitivity to national developments. The index numbers are ranked accordingly, with the highest index receiving the number one ranking. The weight factor applied is 5 percent.

The ninth indicator, I, is also related to local-national employment linkages (basic industry status). As determined through the calculation of coefficients of specialization, each industry in the local economy is determined to be either basic (export) or nonbasic (local service). Basic industries are considered to be the prime employment generators of the local economy and, as such, create additional employment and income for the local area. As a consequence, the prosperity of the nonbasic sectors of the local economy is dependent upon the prosperity of the basic industries. In this capacity, then, base industries are those which tend to be the leaders of local economic performance. If job opportunities are arising in the local economy, they are probably linked to growth in the basic industries. It is the interrelated nature of the basic versus nonbasic sectors of the local economy which allows base industry status to be given a more favorable position in a relative evaluative model. If an industry has a coefficient of specialization of 1.00 or greater, it is considered basic and awarded 10 points. When the quotient is less than 1.00, the industry is classified as nonbasic and given 30 points. These point scores are multiplied by a weight factor of 5 percent.

The Complete Model

The final numerical process is relatively simple. Using the Industry Evaluative Model, the appropriate rankings or point totals are inserted into their respective slots in the equation. For any given industry (SIC):

Industry Evaluation Quotient $= .20(A) + .20(B) + .10(C) + .10(D) + .10(E) + .10(F) + .10(G) + .05(H) + .05(I)$

Because seven of the nine input variables are rank orders, the model evaluates the relative position of each industry in the local economy. When the weight factors are applied to each rank ordered variable, the ranking of that industry is magnified by the weight factors. Since the model weights high employment levels and large increases in employment more heavily, larger industries are given greater priority. The industry with the *lowest* Industry Evaluation Quotient (IEQ) is ranked number one and thereby is classified as the industry with the greatest relative potential for job opportunity.

Results

The data for Austin/Travis County have been inserted into the industry evaluation model; results appear in table A3-2. For the sake of consistency, all of the two-digit industries which have been examined throughout the industry analysis are shown. Table A3-3 depicts the Industrial Evaluation Quotients and the rank order of each industry as it moves from the industry with the best employment potential to the last entry which has the least relative employment potential.

With few exceptions, the results are consistent with the more qualitative data review in the first four analytical steps. It is noteworthy that only the top three or four ranked industries can be selected by a careful perusal of the data, while the Industry Evaluation Model ranks *all* of the industries under study.

Table A3-2
Industrial Evaluation

| | | | RANK ORDERS | | --- | | RANK ORDERS | | | | RANKED |
SIC#	INDUSTRY	LOCAL EMPLY	CHANGE EMPLY	EMPLY PROJ	81 BUS ESTAB	CHANGE ESTAB	JOB POINTS	POT NEW HIRES	AG HOUR INDEX	BAS IND POINTS	IND EVAL QUOTIENT	IND EVAL QUOTIENT
1	AG CROPS	45	22	70	11	69	5	4	46	30	33.1	40
2	AG LIVESTOCK	40	13	69	4	19	5	7	45	30	24.75	25
7	AG SERVICES	44	40	38	25	15	1	14	44	10	28.8	32
9	FISH,HUNT,TRAP	70	61	68	70	61	5	70	43	30	57.25	70
10	METAL MINING	69	64	67	69	66	5	61	9	30	55.35	67
13	OIL & GAS EXT	48	35	43	34	18	5	37	26	30	33.1	39
14	NONMETAL MINERAL	63	58	50	65	56	5	60	59	30	52.25	63
15	GEN BUILDING CON	11	7	24	8	3	1	5	61	10	11.25	8
16	HEAVY CON	24	15	14	28	14	1	32	68	10	20.6	17
17	SPCL TRADE CON	4	4	10	1	6	1	1	62	10	7.1	4
20	FOOD & KINDRED	33	39	42	45	46	5	51	58	30	37.7	46
22	TEXTILE MILL	68	66	66	68	60	5	69	30	30	56.6	69
23	APPAREL	59	54	57	58	45	5	64	23	30	48.15	58
24	LUMBER & WOOD	43	32	47	42	39	1	42	49	30	36.05	44
25	FURN & FIX	37	34	65	53	55	5	54	22	10	39	47
26	PAPER PROD	60	55	64	64	53	5	68	24	30	51.1	61
27	PRINT & PUB	19	24	26	22	13	3	33	13	10	19.45	15
28	CHEMICALS	41	20	11	52	40	5	47	18	30	30.1	34
29	PETROLEUM & COAL	62	57	63	61	50	5	66	57	30	52.65	65
30	RUBBER & PLASTIC	57	68	56	54	64	4	56	8	30	50.3	59
31	LEATHER	64	65	62	66	63	5	67	55	30	56.35	68
32	STONE,CLAY,GLASS	36	33	37	46	49	4	50	52	10	35.5	43
33	PRIMARY METAL	58	52	53	63	59	5	52	4	30	46.9	57
34	FABRICATED METAL	35	28	33	36	33	4	45	12	30	29.8	33
35	MACH,EX,ELECTRIC	5	70	5	38	43	4	22	1	10	26.75	29
36	ELEC & ELEC EQUP	6	5	1	40	32	3	25	6	10	13.1	10
37	TRANS EQUIP	56	69	35	57	52	5	46	5	30	46.25	56
38	INSTRUMENTS	30	43	23	49	44	5	38	15	10	31.75	37
39	MISC MANUFAC	42	41	46	48	48	5	55	37	30	40.15	48
41	LOCAL & INTURBAN	47	50	45	56	62	5	57	38	30	45.3	55
42	TRUCKING & WH	34	36	40	26	30	2	30	50	30	30.8	36
44	WATER TRANSPORT	67	62	61	60	51	5	63	69	30	54.75	66
45	AIR TRANSPORT	49	37	52	51	47	5	58	70	30	43.5	54

Table A3-2 (cont.)

SIC#	INDUSTRY	LOCAL EMPLY	RANK ORDERS CHANGE EMPLY	EMPLY PROJ	81 BUS ESTAB	CHANGE ESTAB	JOB POINTS	RANK ORDERS POT NEW HIRES	AG HOUR INDEX	BAS IND POINTS	IND EVAL QUOTIENT	RANKED IND EVAL QUOTIENT
46	PIPELINES	66	60	60	62	58	5	59	14	30	51.8	62
47	TRANSPORT SERV	54	46	55	35	20	4	48	63	30	40.85	51
48	COMMUNICATION	18	42	17	44	27	5	40	40	10	27.8	31
49	ELEC & GAS	50	45	32	55	68	1	43	29	30	41.85	52
50	WHLSALE TRADE D	7	6	9	9	9	1	16	17	10	8.35	5
51	WHLSALE TRADE ND	22	25	29	19	23	3	28	34	30	22.8	20
52	BUILDING MATS	28	27	28	27	25	3	31	36	10	24.7	24
53	GEN MERCHANDISE	12	14	18	50	67	1	49	48	30	27.6	30
54	FOOD STORES	8	8	7	24	31	3	26	32	10	14.4	11
55	AUTO DEALERS	15	23	20	16	70	3	12	21	10	21.25	19
56	APPAREL & ACC'ES	23	67	22	21	29	3	20	47	10	30.35	35
57	FURN - RETAIL	29	26	39	20	16	3	24	28	10	23.1	21
58	EAT & DRINK PL	1	1	3	6	8	1	2	53	10	5.55	2
59	MISC RETAIL	10	9	12	7	7	1	9	33	10	9.55	6
60	BANKING	20	30	25	43	26	4	35	25	30	26.05	27
61	CREDIT AGENCIES	26	18	34	30	34	5	39	16	10	24.3	23
62	SEC/COM BROKERS	52	47	54	41	24	3	53	39	30	40.75	50
63	INSURANCE CARR	14	12	16	29	28	5	10	20	10	15.5	12
64	INSUR BROKERS	32	31	41	18	12	4	29	64	10	26.7	28
65	REAL ESTATE	13	11	13	5	2	1	6	67	10	11.35	9
66	COMBO RE,INS	61	63	59	59	65	5	62	3	10	50.45	60
67	HOLDING OFFICES	53	48	44	37	42	5	41	60	10	40.6	49
70	HOTELS	16	10	19	33	41	1	23	51	10	19.95	16
72	PERS SERVICES	21	17	31	14	37	3	13	65	10	21.15	18
73	BUS SERVICES	2	2	2	2	1	1	3	7	10	2.55	1
75	AUTO REPAIR	31	29	36	17	38	3	15	10	10	23.9	22
76	MISC REPAIR	46	38	51	31	22	5	36	19	30	33.75	41
78	MOTION PICTURES	55	56	49	47	36	5	44	31	30	43.35	53
79	AMUSEMENT & REC	39	44	30	32	54	5	21	41	30	34.35	42
80	HEALTH SERVICES	3	21	6	3	5	1	8	27	30	9.95	7
81	LEGAL SERVICES	27	16	27	12	11	4	17	11	10	16.75	13
82	EDUC SERVICES	38	51	48	39	35	2	34	35	30	36.85	45
83	SOCIAL SERVICES	17	19	8	23	17	2	19	56	10	17.4	14
84	MUSEUMS	65	59	58	67	57	5	65	42	10	52.6	64
86	MEMBERSHIP ORGS	25	49	15	13	21	3	11	66	30	25.9	26
88	PRIV HOUSEHOLDS	51	53	21	15	10	5	27	54	10	31.8	38
89	MISC SERVICES	9	3	4	10	4	3	18	2	10	6.9	3

Table A3-3
Industrial Evaluation Quotients

SIC#	INDUSTRY	QUOTIENT	RANK ORDER	SIC#	INDUSTRY	QUOTIENT	RANK ORDER
73	BUS SERVICES	2.55	1	38	INSTRUMENTS	31.75	37
58	EAT & DRINK PL	5.55	2	88	PRIV HOUSEHOLDS	31.8	38
89	MISC SERVICES	6.9	3	13	OIL & GAS EXT	33.1	39
17	SPCL TRADE CON	7.1	4	1	AG CROPS	33.1	40
50	WHLSALE TRADE D	8.35	5	76	MISC REPAIR	33.75	41
59	MISC RETAIL	9.55	6	79	AMUSEMENT & REC	34.35	42
80	HEALTH SERVICES	9.95	7	32	STONE,CLAY,GLASS	35.5	43
15	GEN BUILDING CON	11.25	8	24	LUMBER & WOOD	36.05	44
65	REAL ESTATE	11.35	9	82	EDUC SERVICES	36.85	45
36	ELEC & ELEC EQUP	13.1	10	20	FOOD & KINDRED	37.7	46
54	FOOD STORES	14.4	11	25	FURN & FIX	39	47
63	INSURANCE CARR	15.5	12	39	MISC MANUFAC	40.15	48
81	LEGAL SERVICES	16.75	13	67	HOLDING OFFICES	40.6	49
83	SOCIAL SERVICES	17.4	14	62	SEC/COM BROKERS	40.75	50
27	PRINT & PUB	19.45	15	47	TRANSPORT SERV	40.85	51
70	HOTELS	19.95	16	49	ELEC & GAS	41.85	52
16	HEAVY CON	20.6	17	78	MOTION PICTURES	43.35	53
72	PERS SERVICES	21.15	18	45	AIR TRANSPORT	43.5	54
55	AUTO DEALERS	21.25	19	41	LOCAL & INTURBAN	45.3	55
51	WHLSALE TRADE ND	22.8	20	37	TRANS EQUIP	46.25	56
57	FURN - RETAIL	23.1	21	33	PRIMARY METAL	46.9	57
75	AUTO REPAIR	23.9	22	23	APPAREL	48.15	58
61	CREDIT AGENCIES	24.3	23	30	RUBBER & PLASTIC	50.3	59
52	BUILDING MATS	24.7	24	66	COMBO RE,INS	50.45	60
2	AG LIVESTOCK	24.75	25	26	PAPER PROD	51.1	61
86	MEMBERSHIP ORGS	25.9	26	46	PIPELINES	51.8	62
60	BANKING	26.05	27	14	NONMETAL MINERAL	52.25	63
64	INSUR BROKERS	26.7	28	84	MUSEUMS	52.6	64
35	MACH,EX,ELECTRIC	26.75	29	29	PETROLEUM & COAL	52.65	65
53	GEN MERCHANDISE	27.6	30	44	WATER TRANSPORT	54.75	66
48	COMMUNICATION	27.8	31	10	METAL MINING	55.35	67
7	AG SERVICES	28.8	32	31	LEATHER	56.35	68
34	FABRICATED METAL	29.8	33	22	TEXTILE MILL	56.6	69
28	CHEMICALS	30.1	34	9	FISH,HUNT,TRAP	57.25	70
56	APPAREL & ACC'ES	30.35	35				
42	TRUCKING & WH	30.8	36				

Other Issues

A final note should be included as a caveat for those who are interested in employing the Industry Evaluation Model. Although this model has proven to be effective for industrial ranking, it is merely a prototype and does not take into consideration peculiar local relationships. For any given local area, the weight factors should be adjusted to reflect local economic conditions. The model may be modified to include additional economic indicators, or other indicators may be substituted for those included in the model. Perhaps the most important point to be made throughout industry employment analysis is that the myriad of industrial data can be *organized* and synthesized to provide valuable information concerning the nature of a local economy. By utilizing this or some other methodology to analyze industry data, the user will be able to identify the economic structure and trends within a specific local area.

After IEQs have been calculated for all the industries under study and each has been appropriately ranked, the analyst should select several of the top industries and identify actual *employers* which constitute those industries in the local area. The identification of firm names and addresses is the culminating step following industry analysis. This can be accomplished by referring to a local directory of manufacturers, a Chamber of Commerce industrial directory, Dun and Bradstreet listings of headquartered firms, or any locally compiled list which can be referenced through an SIC category index.

Appendix 4
Economic Base Analysis
and the Local Economy

That group of industries which generates the greatest amount of employment and income in excess of the needs of the local community is referred to as the economic base. Economic base analysis, as previously mentioned, is a tool for identifying those industries which are the keys to the local economy. The industries with the highest and therefore most significant coefficients of specialization in a given local economy comprise the area's base industries and are the cornerstones of the local economy. In analyzing the area's economic base, the diversity of the local economy and its business cycle sensitivity can be uncovered. Base analysis serves two main purposes: (1) to identify the major current sources of income and employment in the local area, and (2) to anticipate the changes in the local area economic structure, both those that will tend to occur naturally and those that should be encouraged in the development of a diversified industrial base.

Where an area specializes in a certain type of industrial activity, e.g., Austin/Travis County and electronic components manufacturing, this concentration tends to perpetuate the further economic development of that industry in that particular area. Large existing concentrations of firms in a particular manufacturing industry, for example, assure the creation and maintenance of a skilled and trained labor force from which to draw. The significance of a skilled labor pool, especially in an area which comprises a large industrial and household market, is well documented in literature relating to industrial relocation. Aside from the labor pool, existing subsidiary and support services have usually been established which provide new firms with experienced subcontractors and finance, distribution, and marketing firms familiar with the needs and problems related to the particular industry. This existing infrastructure can lead to agglomeration economies which tend to lessen both long and short run costs to a new manufacturer in that industry. Therefore, expansion tends to come in those industries which already exist in an area, increasing the concentration of firms in a particular industry and making the economic base of the local area less diversified and more dependent on a single or a few industrial sectors. Although such concentration or dependence is not inherently bad, the local economy becomes extremely sensitive to the prosperity or decline of the particular key industry(s). Should such a key or base industry suffer serious declines in demand and production, the local economy loses the employment and income generated by that industry. Where the local economy is not sufficiently diversified to absorb the employment and income losses caused by the demise of a key industry, that economy will suffer severe recessionary effects. Such key industry declines have recently affected many of the traditional midwestern manufacturing areas such as Akron, Ohio and Flint, Michigan, which have suffered the economic hardships that can occur in a nondiversified local economy when the key industry declines.

Not only does the local economy lose the income and jobs generated by the key industry, but such a loss triggers a series of losses in those firms and industries which are economically dependent on the key industry. This so-called multiplier or "ripple" effect occurs when the key industry has reduced its production to the point that it must reduce its work force through layoffs, and reduce the amount of related subcontract and service business it previously generated. If the economy is not diverse enough to supply new business opportunities, subcontractors and service firms will also be forced to lay off workers.

This first wave or ripple results in increasing the number of unemployed and reducing the production of goods which can be potentially sold for revenue. The second ripple occurs when those individuals who have been laid off no longer have as much money to spend on personal goods and services. Collectively, they buy fewer groceries, stop going to the movies, put off buying new clothes and appliances, and drive the old car that much longer. As the scenario unfolds in the local economy, the second ripple of reduced spending by individuals triggers a new decline in sales and services in other firms and industries. These declines in demand result in more layoffs which continue the ripples through the local and regional economy. Although this is a highly simplified explanation of the "multiplier effect," it does point out the importance of the key industries in each local area and the need for a diversified economy to avoid or offset the potential effect from the decline of a key industry.

Identifying the Economic Base

Economic base analysis describes all productive activity in terms of two categories: basic or base activities which sell in export markets and bring additional employment and revenue into the local area, and service or nonbasic activities whose output is consumed totally within the local area. The importance of economic base theory is in its ability to identify those basic sectors of a local economy which will bring growth, in terms of revenues and employment, into the local area. This exogenous expansion will in turn cause local service sectors to expand and prosper in accordance with the multiplier concept of regenerative expansion. It is the basic industries which hold the key to local expansion, and therefore identifying those sectors of the local economy which are base and monitoring their change provides a predictive tool for general regional changes. One technique which can be applied to analysis of the local economic base is called the location quotient approach, and identifies basic sectors by comparing the local area's consumption patterns with those of the nation. A coefficient of specialization can be computed in accordance with the location quotient approach to determine a region's basic industrial sector(s). The equation for the coefficient of specialization can be written:

Coefficient of Specialization =

$$\frac{\text{Regional Employment in Industry i}}{\text{Total Regional Employment}} \div \frac{\text{National Employment in Industry i}}{\text{Total National Employment}}$$

For a given geographical area defined by the planner, employment by industry must be obtained for some given year. The next step involves an assumption that local (regional) residents have the same demand patterns as those on a national level. In other words, a planner must treat the national economy as a total local (regional) sector which provides a comparison figure for the local (regional) level. Thus if the local (regional) area is completely self-sufficient in one industrial group (that is, it neither exports nor imports products in that industrial group), we would expect that local (regional) employment in that industry as a percent of total local (regional) employment would be the same as national employment in that industry as a percent of total national employment.

An index number is calculated for each industrial group (or occupational group). If the percent employment in an industry or occupation at the local (regional) level is exactly the same as the percent employment of the industry or occupation at the national level, the index would be 1.00. If it is greater, the index number will be greater than 1.00; if it is less, the index number will be less than 1.00. The employment in those industries with coefficients greater than 1.00 is then designated as basic employment, and those industries with coefficients of less than 1.00 are designated as nonbasic or service employment.

Coefficients of specialization can be computed for employment by industry and employment by occupation. By computing the coefficients for different time periods, a planner may obtain an idea of whether the area is becoming more or less specialized economically. In this manner a planner can be aware of the impact of economic policies on the employment status of individuals in various industries. The process is highly simplistic, however, and reasoned judgment should be used in its application.

DEMCO